Folklore of the

North American Indians

AN ANNOTATED BIBLIOGRAPHY

COMPILED BY Judith C. Ullom

Children's Book Section
General Reference and Bibliography Division

LIBRARY OF CONGRESS · WASHINGTON · 1969

A woodcut from Once Upon a Totem *by Christie Harris has been adapted for the cover and frontispiece of this book. The illustrator, John Frazer Mills, based his woodcuts on the Indian art of the Pacific Northwest. Eagle and Raven, shown on page 47, are characters in Indian tales as well as symbolic figures in totem art. Item 65.*

The halftitles are indicated by the silhouette of a deer, reproduced from When Coyote Walked the Earth, *a collection of tales written by Corinne Running and illustrated by Richard Bennett. Item 68.*

The border of stylized birds that introduces each chapter is reproduced from Zuñi Folk Tales *collected by Frank Hamilton Cushing. The frieze-like decoration by an unknown illustrator appears at the end of "The Youth and His Eagle." Item 129.*

L.C. Card 70–601462

For sale by the Superintendent of Documents
Government Printing Office
Washington, D. C. 20402   Price $2.25

In the vast accumulation of recorded folklore, including much that is important to children for their reading and to storytellers for their repertoires, are many tales of the North American Indians. Stith Thompson calls them "by far the most extensive body of tales representative of any primitive people," coming down to us in Government reports, folklore journals, and publications of learned societies. This bibliography aims to reveal a selection from these extensive resources.

By the end of the 19th century—with the development of the Bureau of American Ethnology; the work of the American Folklore Society, museums, and universities; and the appearance of the *Journal of American Folklore*—a systematic effort was being made to preserve the oral heritage of the Indian. Record-making expeditions of trained ethnologists and anthropologists followed the collecting done by Indian agents, missionaries, traders, and others who lived and hunted with the Indians. Both groups preserved traditional lore as they heard it from tribal storytellers. Later collections such as *John Rattling-Gourd of Big Cove* (item 125) have been gathered from folklore still living today, thus making accessible valuable new source books of stories often reported to be told to tribal children. Other compilers reworked tales they found by searching through folklore journals and expedition reports. Anthropologist Melville Jacobs made a plea that "Our indigenous oral literatures can and should be available, with suitable changes in content and style, to the Europeans who have entered and made their homes on the new continents. The richness as well as the variety of the literatures and cultural heritages of the American Indians can be introduced to children" (*When Coyote Walked the Earth*, item 68).

The tales with which we are concerned here were gathered from widespread locations, across North America from Alaska to the Northeast, the Southeast, and the Southwest. Eleven culture areas, including the Eskimo, are outlined on a map reproduced from folklorist Stith Thompson's *Tales of the North American Indians* (item 16). In the present bibliography items representing these 11 culture areas are arranged according to the order set forth by Mr. Thompson, with editions for children following each section of source materials.

Spellings of tribal names are those established by the Library of Congress after consideration of John R. Swanton's *The Indian Tribes of North America* (Washington, U.S. Govt. Print. Off., 1952. 726 p.), *Bulletin* 145 of the Bureau of American Ethnology of the Smithsonian Institution. For names of mythological characters such as Glooscap and Manabozho the spelling conforms to that of the author of the work described.

The types of tales found in most areas can be described as myths—which account for natural phenomena and the characteristics of living creatures and inanimate objects—hero cycles, and trickster tales. Knud Rasmussen has classified the Eskimo tales as "epic, religious, humorous, and soporific," claiming that the "soporific tales were merely intended for passing the time away and by means of sleep getting people through the long waiting of the winter months. In relating them the teller adopts a monotonous and lethargic form calculated to put his audience to sleep in a very short time."

This bibliography does not aim to be comprehensive. Criteria for choosing the best materials for the compiler or reteller of these folktales, for the storyteller or librarian serving children, and for the child's own reading are (1) statement of sources and faithfulness to them, (2) a true reflection of Indian cosmology, and (3) a written style that retains the spirit and poetry of the Indian's native manner of telling. Some of the source materials are included because they contain valuable introductory materials, bibliographies, motif indexes, and additional comparative notes.

Call numbers indicate location of the items in the Library of Congress collections.

The Children's Book Section gratefully acknowledges the valuable consultative services of Dr. William H. Gilbert, Jr., specialist in Indian affairs, Library of Congress; Miss Elva Van Winkel, Public Library of the District of Columbia; and Mrs. Marjorie Halpin, docent in anthropology, Smithsonian Institution.

Virginia Haviland
Head, Children's Book Section
General Reference and Bibliography Division
Reference Department

Contents

Foreword   v

Acknowledgments   ix

GENERAL BACKGROUND

The Primitive Folktale   3
Studies   4
Anthologies   9
Children's Anthologies   15
Bibliographies and Indexes   17

NORTH AMERICAN CULTURE AREAS

Eskimo   21
Mackenzie   32
Plateau   35
North Pacific   40
California   52
Plains   60
Central Woodland   73
Northeast Woodland   83
Iroquois   90
Southeast   94
Southwest   100

Index   121

Acknowledgments

The illustration used as cover and frontispiece and that on page 47, both by John Frazer Mills from *Once Upon a Totem* by Christie Harris, copyright © 1963 by Christie Harris, are reproduced by permission of Atheneum Publishers.

The illustration used on the halftitles and that on page 51, both by Richard Bennett from *When Coyote Walked the Earth; Indian Tales of the Pacific Northwest* by Corinne Running, copyright 1949 by Corinne Running, are reproduced by permission of Holt, Rinehart and Winston, Inc.

The illustration on page 2 and that at the beginning of each chapter, from *Zuñi Folk Tales* by Frank Hamilton Cushing, copyright 1931 by Alfred A. Knopf, Inc., are reproduced by permission of Alfred A. Knopf, Inc.

The illustration on page 10 and the music on page 11, from *The Indians' Book* by Natalie Curtis, are reproduced by permission of Dover Publications, Inc., who reprinted the volume in 1969.

The map on page 14, from *Tales of the North American Indians* by Stith Thompson, is reproduced by permission of Indiana University Press.

The illustrations on pages 29 and 30, by Carol Jones from *The Day Tuk Became a Hunter & Other Eskimo Stories* by Ronald Melzack, © 1967 by Ronald Melzack, and those on pages 85 and 89, by Robert Frankenberg from *Glooscap and His Magic; Legends of the Wabanaki Indians* by Kay Hill, copyright © 1963 by Kay Hill, are reproduced by permission of Dodd, Mead & Company, Inc.

The illustration on pages 34 and 35, by Dorothy McEntee from *Nine Tales of Coyote* by Frances Martin, copyright 1950 by Harper & Brothers, and that on pages 48 and 49, by Dorothy McEntee from *Nine Tales of Raven* by Frances Martin, copyright 1951 by Harper & Brothers, are reproduced by permission of Harper & Row, Publishers.

The illustration on page 56, by Enrico Arno from *Down From the Lonely Mountain; California Indian Tales* by Jane Louise Curry, © 1965 by Jane Louise Curry, is reproduced by permission of Harcourt, Brace & World, Inc.

x   The illustrations on pages 58 and 59, by Ruth Robbins from *Stories California Indians Told* by Anne B. Fisher, copyright 1957 by Anne B. Fisher for text, by Ruth Robbins for illustrations, are reproduced by permission of Parnassus Press.

The illustration on pages 68 and 69, by Charles M. Russell from Frank B. Linderman's *Indian Why Stories,* copyright 1915 by Charles Scribner's Sons, is reproduced by permission of Charles Scribner's Sons.

The illustration on page 71 by Roland Whitehorse from *Winter-Telling Stories* by Alice Marriott, copyright 1947 by William Sloane Associates, Inc., is reproduced with permission.

The illustration on page 72, by Walter Richard West from *Tales of the Cheyennes* by Grace Jackson Penney, copyright 1953 by Grace Jackson Penney; that on pages 116 and 117, by Virginia Lee Burton from *Don Coyote* by Leigh Peck, copyright 1942 by Leigh Peck; and that on page 119, by John P. Heins from *Navaho Tales* by William Whitman 3rd, copyright 1925 by William Whitman 3rd, are reproduced by permission of Houghton Mifflin Company.

The illustrations on pages 78 and 79, by Yeffe Kimball from *The World of Manabozho; Tales of the Chippewa Indians* by Thomas B. Leekley, copyright © 1965 by Thomas B. Leekley, are reproduced by permission of Vanguard Press, Inc.

The illustration on page 81, by Donald Grant from *Tales of Nanabozho* by Dorothy M. Reid, © Oxford University Press 1963, is reproduced by permission of Henry C. Walck, Inc.

The illustration on page 98, from *John Rattling-Gourd of Big Cove; a Collection of Cherokee Indian Legends,* written and illustrated by Corydon Bell, copyright 1955 by The Macmillan Company, is reproduced by permission of The Macmillan Company.

The illustrations on pages 102 and 104, from *The Kachinas Are Coming; Pueblo Indian Kachina Dolls With Related Folktales,* written and illustrated by Gene Meany Hodge, copyright 1936 by Steller-Millar, are reproduced by permission of the author.

The illustration on page 109, from *Indian Tales of the Desert People,* written and illustrated by William D. Hayes, copyright 1957 © by William D. Hayes, is reprinted by permission of David McKay Company, Inc.

The illustration on page 118, by Katherine F. Kitt from *Long Ago Told Legends of the Papago Indians* by Harold Bell Wright, copyright 1929 by D. Appleton and Company, is reproduced by permission of Meredith Press.

General Background

The Primitive Folktale

References in this section present an overall picture of North American Indian mythology and folklore. Studies of the following topics are listed: the folktale in a primitive culture, the stylistic aspects of primitive literature, comparative discussions of literary form in the New World and the Old, and summaries of important myths presented in relation to the cultures they interpret. These studies also discuss the role of the storyteller since early times in reworking his material artistically and adapting it to the demands of his audience.

The anthologies offer examples of some of the best of the North American Indian tales gathered from hard-to-come-by scholarly works. Three of these collections incorporate material from the quarterly *Journal of American Folklore* (v. 1+ Apr./June 1888+ Philadelphia, American Folklore Society. GR1.J8), which in 1888 set forth as one of its stated purposes the "collection of the fast-vanishing remains of Folk-Lore in America." Folklore journals have not been analyzed for this bibliography, but they are listed in *Folklore for Children and Young People* (item 22) and other items in this section. Among the separately published bibliographies are one that attempts to be complete in bringing together authentic material, popular collections, and editions for children (item 20), and one that is selective, with critical annotations by a folklore specialist (item 22).

Among the many native storytellers who have contributed to a knowledge of Indian folklore was Waíhusiwa, a Zuñi. He told the story "The Serpent of the Sea," recorded in Frank Hamilton Cushing's Zuñi Folk Tales, and his portrait is reproduced from the same volume. Item 129.

1. Alexander, Hartley B.
   North American [mythology]. New York, Cooper Square Publishers, 1964 [c1916] 325 p. illus., maps (1 fold. mounted on cover),
   33 plates (part col.) (The Mythology of all races, v. 10)
                                                            BL25.M8 1964, v. 10

   Bibliography: p. [313]–325.

   A professor of philosophy summarizes for the general reader important myths of each culture area north of Mexico; they were selected
   from a vast body of material collected by students of anthropology.
   Each chapter summarizes the life and culture of an area and discusses
   its important linguistic stocks and the myths that characterize their
   concept of the universe. This arrangement illustrates the author's introductory discussion of myth with reference to source and motive.

2. Boas, Franz.
   Race, language and culture. New York. Macmillan, 1940. 647 p.
   illus., tables, diagrs.   GN8.B68

   Bibliographical footnotes.

   A noted American anthropologist's selected writings on the mythology
   and folklore of the Indian and the Eskimo allow the nonspecialist to
   discover the distinctive quality of primitive literature in the New
   World. Dr. Boas shows that the role of the storyteller since early times
   has been to rework his material artistically and adapt it to the demands
   of his audience.

   In "The Development of the Folk-Tales and Myths" (1916) the
   author suggests a process by which plots and incidents have become
   widely distributed throughout many culture areas, where they acquired
   a local character. Dr. Boas' investigation of the content of the myths
   reveals that they probably originated from the play of imagination on
   daily happenings, rather than from primitive man's direct contempla-
   tion of nature.

   "The Growth of Indian Mythologies" (1895) is a study of how dissemination occurs and of factors that influence or inhibit the distribution of a tale.

   "Dissemination of Tales Among the Natives of North America"
   (1891) gives criteria for determining whether a tale is of independent
   origin within a particular tribe or culture area or whether it, with
   others, can be said to have derived from a common source.

   "Mythology and Folk-Tales of the North American Indians" (1914),
   a six-part article, concerns myths, tales, and legends as primitive art.

"Stylistic Aspects of Primitive Literature" (1925) compares the forms in which primitive literature is found in the New World and the Old and shows how the cultural life of a people influences the content and form of its literature.

"The Folk-Lore of the Eskimo" (1925) describes the main characteristics of Eskimo folklore east of the Mackenzie River and outlines some of the important themes.

"Romance Folk-Lore Among American Indians" (1925) shows the extent to which Bible tales and tales of French, Spanish, Portuguese, and Negro origin have been integrated into Indian folklore.

3. Dundes, Alan.
THE MORPHOLOGY OF NORTH AMERICAN INDIAN FOLKTALES. Helsinki, Suomalainen Tiedeakatemia [sold by Akateeminen Kirjakauppa] 1964. 134 p. (FF communication, v. 81, 3, no. 195)

GR1.F55, no. 195

Bibliographical references included in "Notes" (p. [113]–134).

A "scientific" study of a primitive art form, the folktale of the North American Indian. In technical language, Alan Dundes develops his thesis that these folktales are "highly structured." In the following order, portions of the book are devoted to a survey of previous scholarship concerning the structure and morphology of American Indian folktales, a delineation of the structural approach to the study of folktales, and specific structural models and examples.

3a. Egoff, Sheila A.
THE REPUBLIC OF CHILDHOOD; A CRITICAL GUIDE TO CANADIAN CHILDREN'S LITERATURE IN ENGLISH. Toronto, Oxford University Press, 1967. 287 p. illus.

PN1009.A1E3

In her chapter on "Indian Legends" (p. 15–35) this professor of children's literature offers a basic introduction to the stylistic aspects of American Indian legends through detailed discussion of such Canadian collections for children as *Sketco the Raven,* by Robert Ayre; *Once Upon a Totem,* by Christie Harris; *Tales of Nanabozho,* by Dorothy Reid; *Glooscap and His Magic,* by Kay Hill; and others. Topics covered include a description of the culture-hero or transformer, who often accomplishes his work for mankind through trickery and mischief, and an analysis of plot, described as a "mélange of anecdotes rather than a single unified narrative." Examples of the raw material of the anthropologist, comparisons with other mythologies, and direct quotes from anthologies for children illustrate the discussion. Miss Egoff notes that these "legends demand scholarship to make them intelligible, craftsmanship to give them shape, and most of all creative artistry in communicating the freshness, sense of wonder, and directness that represent their greatest appeal to children." In a concluding list are critical annotations of 12 titles.

An article based on this chapter appeared in the journal *In Review, Canadian Books for Children,* winter 1967: 5–15.

4. Garfield, Viola E.
CONTEMPORARY PROBLEMS OF FOLKLORE COLLECTING AND STUDY. *In* Alaska. University. Anthropological papers, v. 1, May 1953: 25–36. illus.   F906.A418, v. 1

An anthropologist discusses the folklore collector's responsibility to present more than just "raw material" if his work is to be of value to others. She suggests that the collector indicate the following: the role of the stories in the lives of the people telling them; how the tales are taught or learned; the degree of freedom a raconteur is allowed, or the artistic framework within which he must stay, in order to be approved by his group; and the extent to which the arrangement of the stories reflects the recorder's own literary tastes. Miss Garfield shows that these and other factors are the dynamics of myth-making, oral literature, and storytelling. A bibliography lists the collections of Indian and Eskimo folklore cited as examples.

5. Hodge, Frederick W., *ed.*
HANDBOOK OF AMERICAN INDIANS NORTH OF MEXICO. New York, Pageant Books, 1960. 2 v. (972, 1221 p.) illus., maps (1 fold.), ports.   E77.H692

Reprint of Bulletin 30 of the Smithsonian Institution, Bureau of American Ethnology.
Bibliography: v. 2, 1179–1221.

This useful encyclopedia, which covers many aspects of Indian mythology, "contains a descriptive list of the stocks, confederacies, tribes, tribal divisions, and settlements north of Mexico, accompanied with the various names by which these have been known, together with biographies of Indians of note, sketches of their history, archaeology, manners, arts, customs, and institutions, and the aboriginal words incorporated into the English language."

6. Jenness, Diamond.
THE INDIANS OF CANADA. 5th ed. [Ottawa] National Museum of Canada [1960] 452 p. illus. (part col.), maps (1 fol. col. in pocket) (National Museum of Canada. Bulletin 65. Anthropological series, no. 15)   QH1.C13, no. 65, 1960

A sourcebook by a noted ethnologist, characterized in the preface as "a comprehensive and authoritative statement valuable alike to the specialist and the layman." Chapters in part 1 describe single traits that relate to material and intellectual culture, including language, economic conditions, and social and political organizations. Two chapters, "Religion" and "Folk-Lore and Traditions," discuss such important topics as the personification of the mysterious forces in nature, supernatural spirits, types of tales and stylistic features, the comparative study of folktales, and dissemination. Part 2 follows a·geographical arrangement; it describes characteristics of the principal tribes of each area and summaries their histories since contact with Europeans.

7. Radin, Paul.
    LITERARY ASPECTS OF NORTH AMERICAN MYTHOLOGY. Ottawa, Govt. Print. Bureau, 1915. 51 p. (Canada. Geological Survey. Museum bulletin no. 16. Anthropological series, no. 6)   QH1.C13, no. 16
                                                                             E98.R3R12

For the storyteller and serious student of folklore, this essay by an anthropologist approaches literary criticism in its detailed analysis of such stylistic elements as thematic material, construction, kinds of actors involved, and situations in which different types of tales are told. By these elements, primitive North American mythology can be characterized as a distinctive literature. Selections from myths of divers tribes illustrate the author's point of view that variability in versions of the same myth can be explained by the variation of one or more stylistic elements and by a narrator's unique artistic instinct to fix the attention of his audience.

8. Thompson, Stith.
    EUROPEAN TALES AMONG THE NORTH AMERICAN INDIANS. *In* Colorado College, Colorado Springs, Colo. Language series. v. 2, 1919: [319]–471.   P25.C6, v. 2

Contents.—The seven-headed dragon.—John the bear.—The wonderful companions.—The enchanted horse.—Little Poucet.—The white cat.—Cinderella; the true bride.—The blue band.—Truth and falsehood.—The wishing ring.—The magic apples.—The magic bird-heart. —The marooned rescuer.—The animal brothers.—Making the princess laugh.—Out-riddling the princess.—Jack the numbskull.—Jack the trickster.—The master thief.--The lucky boaster.—The anger bargain.—Strong John.—Animal stories.—Fables.—Bible stories.—Miscellaneous tales.—Other stories.—Results of study.

Mr. Thompson's study, according to the introduction, is "strictly limited in its scope. It attempts no solution of the problem of remote parallels in tales or of possible pre-Columbian contact with the Old World. It seeks rather, in connection with such versions of European tales as have been admitted to the body of Indian legend, to display clearly their relation to the well-known originals as seen in the great French, French Canadian, German, or Spanish collections. It tries to show by concrete examples how the material of folk-tales behaves under a different environment from that which gave it birth."

The author gives summary outlines of well-known European folk-tales and outlines of Indian versions that are direct borrowings from definite European cycles. Sources for all versions are cited.

9. ————.

THE FOLKTALE. New York, Dryden Press, 1946. 510 p.

PN1001.T5

"Important works on the folktale": p. 463–479.

Contents.—pt. 1. Nature and forms of the folktale.—pt. 2. The folk-tale from Ireland to India (the complex tale, the simple tale, the folktale in ancient literature, European Asiatic folktales in other continents).—pt. 3. The folktale in a primitive culture: North American Indian (creation myths, the trickster cycle, test and hero tales, journeys to the other world, animal wives and husbands, and miscellaneous tales).—pt. 4. Studying the folktale (theories, international organization of folktale study, collecting, classifying, the life history of a folktale, and the folktale as living art).

In a scholarly study, this authority discusses the importance of folk-tales, their history, and their dissemination. Part 3, "The North American Indian Tale," begins with a brief historical survey of the early source material and the contribution of such pioneer collectors as Henry Rowe Schoolcraft, followed by a list of the principal geographic groupings, defined as culture areas, of American Indian tribes in which a common type of narrative has developed. For each main class of Indian tales, those of a number of culture areas are described and discussed.

The volume concludes with "Important Works on the Folktale, Principal Collections of Folktales," by continent and country; "Index of Tale Types," that is, animal, ordinary, jokes and anecdotes, each with subdivisions; and "Index of Motifs," such as mythological, animals, tabu, magic, the dead, marvels, ogres, tests, the wise and the foolish, deceptions, and reversal of fortune.

10. Wissler, Clark.

THE AMERICAN INDIAN, AN INTRODUCTION TO THE ANTHROPOLOGY OF THE NEW WORLD. 3d ed. New York, P. Smith, 1950. 466 p. illus., maps (1 fold.)   E58.W832

Contents.—The food areas of the New World.—Domestication of animals and methods of transportation. . . .—The textile arts.—The ceramic arts.—Decorative designs.—Architecture.—Work in stone and metals.—Special inventions.—The fine arts.—Social grouping.—Social regulation.—Ritualistic observances.—Mythology.—The classification of social groups according to their cultures.—Archaeological classification.—Chronology of cultures.—Linguistic classification.—Somatic classification.—New World origins.—Appendix.

Prepared by the Curator of Anthropology in the American Museum of Natural History, New York, this basic handbook summarizes the results of anthropological research in the New World; it covers economic life, material culture, and art. Chapters 1 through 13 present a general review of the most significant single traits of culture. Briefly stated in chapter 13, "Mythology," are the results of such specialized studies as Robert Lowie's "The Test-Theme in North American Mythology" (*Journal of American Folklore,* v. 21, Apr.–Sept. 1908: [97]–148), and Thomas Waterman's "The Explanatory Element in the Folk-Tales of the North-American Indians" (*Journal of American Folklore,* v. 27, Jan.–Mar. 1914: 1–54). The remaining chapters classify tribal groups according to traits shared in common over a wide geographic, that is, culture, area.

Anthologies

11. Burlin, Natalie (Curtis), *ed.*
    THE INDIANS' BOOK: AN OFFERING BY THE AMERICAN INDIANS OF INDIAN LORE, MUSICAL AND NARRATIVE, TO FORM A RECORD OF THE SONGS AND LEGENDS OF THEIR RACE. Illustrations from photographs and from original drawings by Indians. New York, Harper [c1935] 582 p. illus., facsim., plates (part col.), ports.
    E98.F6B96 1935

Includes music.

The songs of the Indian record "the teachings of his wise men, the great deeds of his heroes, the council of his seers, the worship of his God." This collection is an offering of the song and poetry of 18 tribes from 6 culture groupings established by the author: Eastern Indians, Plains Indians, Lake Indians, Northwestern Indians, Southwestern Indians, and Pueblo Indians. Every song is accompanied by an Indian's account "of the event which called it into being, the legend with which it is connected, or the ceremony of which it is a part." Recorded are

In "Lololomai's Prayer," from The Indians' Book, *Natalie Curtis records her farewell visit to Oraibi, a Hopi village. She is told she will be included in the chief's prayers and that when he prays, "He prays for everything that has life." In this full-color painting by V. Shiye, a Cochiti Indian, the circle represents the sun at dawn, which carries the prayers with it in its passage through the day. The symbolic creature at the right, both human and animal, with a prayer feather attached to its forehead, suggests the spiritual relationship of all life to a supreme Power. Item 11.*

traditional songs and songs taken down "from the lips of their own composers," rendered into English so that the "fragrance, the color, and above all, the spirit of the original" Indian poetry are retained. A historical sketch of each tribe, giving a brief description of its traditions and beliefs, accompanies each section. Eloise Ramsey, in *Folklore for Children and Young People* (item 22), considers this work as "indispensable for the study of Indian music. It is also a book in which young people have evinced keen interest." "Wai-Kun" is an example of a song and its story:

Once there were some mice under a crooked log and they believed they were the only people in the whole world. One of them standing up and stretching his little arms could just touch the under side of the log. He thought that he was very tall and that he touched the sky. So he danced and sang this song:

Mo-zhun-na-le,
  Pe-zhe ya-ki-ske shun-non-nink
    na-gi-kche!
Mo-zhun-na-le,
  Pe-zhe ya-ki-ske shun-non-nink
    na-gi-kche!
Ne-sha-na ma-chi-nik-gla ya-ki-o-o!

Throughout the world
Who is there like little me!
  Who is like me!
I can touch the sky,
I touch the sky indeed!

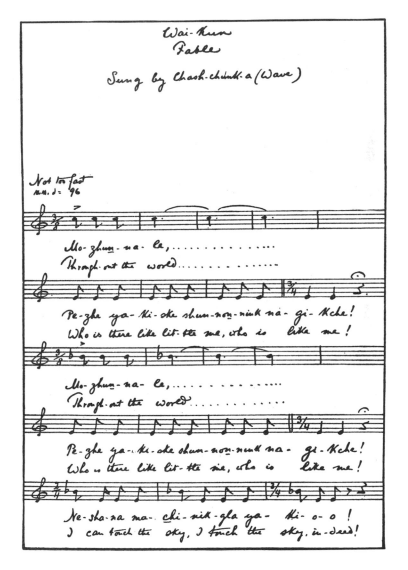

12. Clark, Ella E.
INDIAN LEGENDS OF CANADA. [Toronto] McClelland and Stewart [1960] 177 p.   E98.F6C56
Includes bibliography.

Representative myths, legends, personal narratives, and historical traditions from each of the culture areas of Canada, selected from original sources, provide material of interest to "readers of all ages" and suitable for reading "in families and in schools." Tales that reveal something of the ancient beliefs, ceremonies, and details of everyday life have been preferred to tales from creator-culture-hero-trickster cycles. The introduction describes briefly Indian storytellers and the traditions surrounding their art as recorded by 19th-century travelers and missionaries. Remarks on the popularity of a theme found throughout a single culture area or common to many precede individual tales illustrating that theme. The style of telling is straightforward and unvaried.

Although the editor does not indicate changes made from the original, sources are given for each tale. Readers will want to consult the original versions to sample the flavor of the native literary styles and to gain their fullness of detail. Yet this volume contains a combination of tellable tales and documentation that is of value to the storyteller and folklorist today.

13. Coffin, Tristram P., *ed.*
INDIAN TALES OF NORTH AMERICA; AN ANTHOLOGY FOR THE ADULT READER. Cover illustration by Peter R. Coffin. Philadelphia, American Folklore Society, 1961. 157 p. ([American Folklore Society] Bibliographical and special series, v. 13)   E98.F6C68, v. 13

In "Remarks on Reading the Tales" the compiler, a folklorist "trained in the history of literature," states that "North American Indian tales are usually published in one of two ways: either in hard-to-come-by scholarly works, where they are analyzed and classified; or in children's collections, where they are sentimentalized and emasculated."

Mr. Coffin introduces the adult reader to some of the best North American Indian and Eskimo tales, which can be read as "stories that are 'simply worth reading.' " The geographically representative selections, "set in an earlier era when animals, birds, objects, forces of nature, and the like behaved as human beings behave," are taken from the *Journal of American Folklore* just as the original collector heard them or as he translated them from an Indian tongue. A comparative discussion of Indian narrative technique and Western literary narrative style, and introductions to the individual groups of tales provide a general survey of Indian mythology and folklore. For further study the compiler cites special studies of the Indian narrative. In a final section are "Notes to the Tales," giving exact citations for each tale, original editor, tribe, and the like; "Other Collections of Indian Tales Published by the American Folklore Society"; and an index to "North American Indian Material Included in the Pages of the *Journal of American Folklore*."

14. Curtis, Edward S.
THE NORTH AMERICAN INDIAN; BEING A SERIES OF VOLUMES PIC-TURING AND DESCRIBING THE INDIANS OF THE UNITED STATES, AND ALASKA. Edited by Frederick W. Hodge, foreword by Theodore Roosevelt; field research conducted under the patronage of J. Pierpont Morgan. [Seattle] E. S. Curtis; [Cambridge University Press] 1907–30. 20 v. fronts. (v. 20 col.), plates, ports.   E77.C97

Edward Curtis defines this work, begun in 1898, as "a comprehensive and permanent record of all the important tribes of the United States and Alaska that still retain to a considerable degree their primitive customs and traditions." Tribes of the eastern culture areas receive little attention. From his firsthand experience Mr. Curtis describes, by text and accompanying illustrations, the environment, history, and manner of living of each tribe. The Indian mode of thought is recorded in a sampling of his creation myths, legends, and folklore, gathered directly from the Indians by the compiler and his assistants and presented in a simple, dignified prose style. The appendix in each volume includes a concise "Tribal Summary," a comparative vocabulary, and an index. The tales, not easily accessible here have general appeal.

15. Feldmann, Susan, *ed.*
THE STORYTELLING STONE; MYTHS AND TALES OF THE AMERICAN INDIANS. [New York, Dell Pub. Co., 1965] 271 p. (A Laurel original)   E98.F6F45

Bibliography: p. [268]–271.

The compiler, a teacher of comparative mythology, has chosen for the general reader some of the most characteristic tales of the North American Indian found in "government reports, folklore journals, publications of learned societies, and a few, mostly out-of-print, collections." Her arrangement by tale type—"In the Days of Creation," "Trickster," and "Tales of Heroes, Supernatural Journeys, and other Folktales"— follows closely the arrangement in Stith Thompson's more comprehensive *Tales of the North American Indians* (item 16). Each section includes representative tales from the major culture areas. The introduction, which contains a comparative summary of the myths of each culture area, and the bibliography, which lists basic sources and representative works, add to the usefulness of this collection.

Culture and tribe areas are charted on this foldout map from Tales of the North American Indians *by Stith Thompson. Item 16.*

16. Thompson, Stith, *ed.*

TALES OF THE NORTH AMERICAN INDIANS. Bloomington, Indiana University Press [1966] 386 p. fold. map. (Midland books, MB–91)

E98.F6T32 1966

Contents.—Mythological stories.—Mythical incidents.—Trickster tales. —Hero tales.—Journeys to the other world.—Animal wives and husbands.—Miscellaneous tales.—Tales borrowed from Europeans.— Bible stories.—Notes (Comparative notes; List of motifs discussed in the notes; Sources arranged by culture areas and tribes).

"Full, well-told" examples of the better known tales of the Indian and Eskimo, selected from the extensive body of available material, are given as they originally appeared in government reports, folklore journals, and publications of learned societies; changes are always indicated. The introductory survey describing the varied character of this body of folklore, the comparative notes (p. [271]–360) showing the extent of distribution of tales and motifs, and the bibliography (p. [373]–386) make this a valuable guide to important source materials for each of the culture areas and tribes.

Children's Anthologies

17. Hooke, Hilda M.

THUNDER IN THE MOUNTAINS, LEGENDS OF CANADA. Illustrations by Clare Bice. Toronto, New York, Oxford University Press [1947]

223 p.   E98.F6H6 1947

Bibliography: p. 221–223.

Eleven of these 14 folktales, some of which are stories of the new settlers, are based on Indian sources and represent many sections of Canada including Labrador. A brief introduction giving the local setting leads directly into each tale. The compiler states in her preface that these stories "are based upon legends gathered up in a variety of ways. Some are taken from authentic source material such as the Anthropological series issued by the Canadian Department of Mines; others embody parts of legendary cycles . . . such as the Hiawatha, Glooscap and Nanna-Bijou stories; . . . some were picked up by word of mouth, and some were adapted from existing versions of familiar legends."

The stories are treated "freely" in an informal narrative style, colored with modern embellishments, as in the descriptions of the new coats Wesukechak makes for the animals. "Lynx, had a coat of butter-yellow, with little tufted ear-muffs," "Kakwa the Porcupine, who wanted to be different, walked proudly up and down in a quilled coat of mail that clanked with every step he took, [and] Atik, whose coat was pale cream-buff with dark brown shadows, and upon whose head was fastened a crown of wonderful horns, branched and pointed like bronze candlesticks."

See also item 49, *An Analysis of Coeur d'Alene Indian Myths;* item 57, *The Content and Style of an Oral Literature;* item 98, *The Trickster;* item 99, *Winnebago Hero Cycles;* item 100, *The Culture of the Winnebago.*

18. Leach, Maria.
THE RAINBOW BOOK OF AMERICAN FOLK TALES AND LEGENDS. Illustrated by Marc Simont. Cleveland, World Pub. Co. [1958] 318 p.
GR105.L4

Includes bibliography.

One section of this anthology contains 10 well-chosen North American Indian tales from that many different tribal areas representing the variety of lore belonging to the Americas. The "Author's Notes" identify the written sources for these very brief, concisely told examples. They are humorously illustrated by Marc Simont, some of whose ink line drawings have a color wash.

19. Olcott, Frances J.
THE RED INDIAN FAIRY BOOK FOR THE CHILDREN'S OWN READING AND FOR STORY-TELLERS. With illustrations by Frederick Richardson. Boston, Houghton Mifflin, 1917. 338 p. illus., plates.   E98.F6O4

This compilation brings children simple, colorful versions of stories, each having a tribal designation. They are listed by month in the table of contents. Early collections made by pioneers, including those found in publications of learned societies and institutions, are cited as sources. The editor notes that "most of the tales have been issued for story-tellers in the columns of the *Saturday Magazine* of the *New York Evening Post.*" Chiefly they comprise "nature stories—poetic fancies of the Indians about birds, beasts, flowers, and rocks of our American meadows, prairies and forests. Here also are the tales of the Wind, Rainbow, Sun, Moon, and Stars," arranged interestingly by season, with a subject index provided. "In retelling, all that is coarse, fierce, and irrational has been eliminated as far as possible, and the moral and fanciful elements retained." The results are appealing to younger children, though one must admit that the tales contain some sentimentality and uniformity.

20. Haywood, Charles.
A BIBLIOGRAPHY OF NORTH AMERICAN FOLKLORE AND FOLKSONG.
2d rev. ed. New York, Dover Publications [1961] 2 v. (1301 p.)
maps (on lining papers)   Z5984.U5H32

Contents.—v. 1. The American people north of Mexico, including
Canada.—v. 2. The American Indians north of Mexico, including the
Eskimos.

An "attempt at a thorough bibliography of American folklore and
folksong," in which folklore is defined to encompass such works as
travel books, biographies, and social and cultural histories. The second
volume is useful for its regional approach; the tribes within each culture area are in alphabetical sequence with material for each listed
under the following headings: "Bibliography," "Serial Publications,"
"General Studies and Collections," "Myths and Mythologies," "Belief
—Witchcraft—Magic," "Folktales—Legends," "Customs—Manners,"
"Folk Poetry—Art—Drama—Speech," "Folk Medicine," "Proverbs—
Riddles," and "Games." Folklore and anthropological journals were
indexed from the first issues to about July 1948.

Children's editions, though not identified as such, are listed among
the field-collected texts, literary reworkings, and writings useful for
their cultural context. Included are titles now out of print, some
worthy of reissuance, and literary reworkings of doubtful ethnic integrity and little storytelling appeal.

21. Journal of American folklore.
ANALYTICAL INDEX. v. 1–70; 1888–1957. Philadelphia, American
Folklore Society, 1958. 384 p. (American Folklore Society. Biblio-
graphical and special series, v. 7)   GR1.J8, v. 7

Contents.—pt. 1. Titles of articles, notes, etc.—pt. 2. Authors of articles,
notes, reviews, etc.—pt. 3. Book reviews, by author of book reviewed.—
pt. 4. News and notices.—pt. 5. Subjects and areas in folklore (with 58
subdivisions).—pt. 6. Nationalities and ethnic groups.—pt. 7. Songs
and rimes: titles and first significant lines.—pt. 8. Tales: types, incidents, characters, objects, etc.

This volume is useful whether or not a complete set of the *Journal
of American Folklore* is on hand.

22. Ramsey, Eloise, *comp.*
FOLKLORE FOR CHILDREN AND YOUNG PEOPLE; A CRITICAL AND DE-
SCRIPTIVE BIBLIOGRAPHY FOR USE IN THE ELEMENTARY AND INTER-

MEDIATE SCHOOL. Philadelphia, American Folklore Society, 1952. 110 p. (Publications of the American Folklore Society. Bibliographical series, v. 3)   Z5981.R3, v. 3

Contents.—pt. 1. Books for children and young people—folk tales, folk rhymes, folk songs and singing games; legends and sagas, literary uses.—pt. 2. Selected sources for teachers—folk tales, folk rhymes, folk songs, and folk music; legends, sagas, and epics; folk-lore and mythology; storytelling; folk arts and crafts; and periodicals.

A basic bibliography, international in scope, of authentic folklore materials. Suitability to the taste of young readers and reliable scholarship were used as criteria for good retellings and authenticity. The compiler emphasizes that "authors, editors and compilers must make clear their sources; they must make clear what editing is theirs and where." "Selected Sources for Teachers" includes works essential to an introduction to folklore. Out-of-print references for which "there are no acceptable substitute sources among current publications" are listed in the appendix.

23. Thompson, Stith.

MOTIF-INDEX OF FOLK-LITERATURE; A CLASSIFICATION OF NARRATIVE ELEMENTS IN FOLKTALES, BALLADS, MYTHS, FABLES, MEDIAEVAL ROMANCES, EXEMPLA, FABLIAUX, JEST-BOOKS, AND LOCAL LEGENDS. Rev. and enl. ed. Bloomington, Indiana University Press [1955–58] 6 v.   GR67.T52

A reference work valuable for analyzing and cataloging tales and myths from all over the world. The single motifs, out of which full-fledged narratives are composed, are arranged in 23 divisions. They range from the mythological and the supernatural—for example, creation, animals with human traits—and the realistic—tasks and quests, tales of gambling—to the humorous. Bibliographical references to special treatments, works listing variants, and sources are cited for each motif. Volume 6 is a detailed, alphabetical index.

North American Culture Areas

Eskimo

For many of the Eskimo tribes storytelling is a principal form of entertainment. The shamans, or medicine men, tell of the supernatural powers and beings. Tales recounted more generally are those based on incidents from the everyday life of the people or their ancestors and embellished with traditional elements of the supernatural. The short, simple narratives that the women relate about the birds and animals that once lived and acted as real people are sometimes referred to as the children's stories; this group constitutes only a small portion of the entire body of folklore. The Indian-related Raven tales of the Eskimo account for the existence of all things. Each type of story is represented in editions for children.

24. Boas, Franz.
THE CENTRAL ESKIMO. *In* U.S. *Bureau of American Ethnology.*
Annual report. 6th; 1884/85. Washington, 1888. p. 399–669. illus.,
plates 2–10 (incl. 2 fold. maps)   E51.U55 6th

"Authorities quoted": p. 410–413.
"Poetry and music": p. 648–658.

An important study of the Central Eskimo, based on Dr. Boas' original
research and his analysis of the work of early explorers in this field.
The major part of this report is a detailed account of the geography
of northeastern America, the distribution of tribes there, and their
material culture, habits, and customs. Of special interest to storytellers
and students of folklore is Dr. Boas' account of religious practices and
beliefs supplemented by an entertaining collection, in English, of
Central Eskimo myths and legends. These are followed by a table
comparing them with the tales and traditions found in Greenland and
among other tribes. The discussion of folklore takes up the *tornait*—
the invisible rulers of every object—and Sedna, goddess of the underworld. Versions of the basic myth associated with this remarkable
goddess are quoted in the discussion. One version, narrated in vivid
detail, records the wooing of Sedna by an Arctic seabird:

> Sedna grew up to be a handsome girl and the youths came from all around to
> sue for her hand, but none of them could touch her proud heart. Finally, at the
> breaking up of the ice in the spring a fulmar flew from over the ice and wooed
> Sedna with enticing song. "Come to me," it said; "come into the land of the birds,
> where there is never hunger, where my tent is made of the most beautiful skins. . . ."
> Sedna could not long resist such wooing and they went together over the vast sea.
> When at last they reached the country of the fulmar, after a long and hard journey,
> Sedna discovered that her spouse had shamefully deceived her.

25. ———.
   ———. Introduction by Henry B. Collins. Lincoln, University of
Nebraska Press [1964] 261 p. illus., maps. (A Bison book, BB 196)
                                             E99.E7B66 1964

"Originally published as a part of the Sixth annual report of the
Bureau of Ethnology, Smithsonian Institution, Washington, 1888."
Includes Eskimo music.

Mr. Collins' introduction to this new edition describes Dr. Boas' study
as his "first major contribution to American anthropology and one
of the two first scientific monographs on the Eskimo."

I. The Eskimo of Baffin Land and Hudson Bay [and] II. Second
report on the Eskimo of Baffin Land and Hudson Bay. *In*
American Museum of Natural History, *New York*. Bulletin. v. 15,
1901 and 1907: [1]–570. illus., maps, plates (part col.), tables.
                                                                QH1.A4, v. 15

Dr. Boas states that this study, based on the observations and notes of
others, "supplements and rectifies in very material points" the description in his 1888 report (item 24). Parts 1 and 2, delineating the extent
of borrowing from Indian mythology and folklore, provide background
information on customs, religious ideas, and mythology. The tales are
grouped according to area, from Cumberland Sound to the western
shore of Hudson Bay. Versions of some stories given in item 24 are
here recorded in greater detail; however, these later collections are,
on the whole, generally less appealing. Part 1 lists tales common to
various Eskimo tribes, a printed source for each story (p. 359–361),
and an index of incidents appearing in these tales (p. 361).

27. Nelson, Edward W.
The Eskimo about Bering Strait. *In* U.S. *Bureau of American
Ethnology*. Annual report. 18th; 1896/97. Washington, 1899.
p. 3–518. illus., 107 plates (incl. fold. map)   E51.U55 18th

A lengthy, detailed description of the western Eskimos, their country,
material culture, customs, and traditions, which is based on the study
made from June 1877 to June 1881 by Mr. Nelson, a naturalist. His
treatment of the Eskimo religion and mythology introduces the
"Genesis Myth—The Raven Father," which accounts for the existence
of all things, and the supernatural animals and other beings mentioned
in the legends. Also considered are methods of relating and teaching
the stories. Alaskan folklore includes stories told by the shamans about
supernatural powers and beings, as well as tales based on incidents
from everyday life and embellished with elements of the supernatural.
The Raven cycle is here recorded in satisfying storytelling style. It
incorporates such tales as "The Raven and the Marmot," an example
of the short, simple stories told by women and considered to be meant
especially for children.

28. Rasmussen, Knud J. V.
Eskimo folk-tales. Collected by Knud Rasmussen, edited and
rendered into English by W. Worster, with illustrations by native
Eskimo artists. London, Copenhagen, Gyldendal, 1921. 156 p.
plates.

Selections from a work in Danish published in 1921.

Copies of this work have been reported to the National Union Catalog by the Boston Public Library and the New York Public Library.

Eskimo tales collected in Greenland by a noted Danish explorer and interpreter of Eskimo life and customs. In selecting and editing this lore for the general reader, Mr. Worster has omitted "vague or doubtful passages" but has kept "as closely as possible to the spirit and tone of the originals, working from the Eskimo text and Knud Rasmussen's Danish version." The translator's introduction discusses stylistic aspects of the tales and makes interesting comparisons, in structure, theme, and motif, to well-known European tales. His skillful editing conveys the touching regret of "these poor Eskimo hunters" for the passing of an age of "greater strength and virtue, greater courage and skill." The versions chosen are short, though the narrative is traditionally spun out in telling because "the aim of the Eskimo storyteller is to pass the time during the long hours of darkness." He triumphs when "he can send his hearers to sleep." Although generally lacking in sustained development, the stories have sufficient dramatic incidents and human interest to make them potential material for the storyteller's art. They tell of the coming of man, why the Raven is black, and how the fog came. There are also tales of heroic men and orphan boys capable of supernatural feats.

29. Rink, Hinrich J.
TALES AND TRADITIONS OF THE ESKIMO, WITH A SKETCH OF THEIR HABITS, RELIGION, LANGUAGE AND OTHER PECULIARITIES. Translated from the Danish by the author. Edinburgh and London, W. Blackwood, 1875. 472 p. illus., plates (1 fold.)   E99.E7R55

Danish original published in Copenhagen in 1866.

The tales in this collection were "written down partly by natives, partly by Europeans, from verbal recital of the natives, and in the latter case to a large extent by the author himself," a Danish naturalist and explorer. Most of the tales were collated from more than one version in an attempt to represent the "most popular mode of telling" the story; they were selected from fuller collections published by Mr. Rink in 1866 and 1871. Background information on the Eskimo is presented in the first part of the book and in the introduction to the tales and traditions. Also discussed are the place of storytelling in Greenland culture—"one of the principal amusements and entertainments"—and the methods by which a storyteller, adding a large measure of the supernatural, draws upon the traditional elements from the "ancient tales" to relate adventures of the Eskimo's ancestors. This process gives the Eskimos "an almost unlimited variety at their storytelling entertainments."

30. THULE EXPEDITION. 5th, 1921–1924. v. 1+ no. 1+ 1945+ Copenhagen, Gyldendal.

Important sources for original folklore material, revealing such rich
finds as a coy version of "Why the Bear Is Stumpy-Tailed" in volume 9
and some tales of Kivioq, "one of the best epic tales" and "one that is
typical of Eskimo fantasy," in volume 8, no. 1. These volumes are
part of the published *Report of the Fifth Thule Expedition 1921–24*,
the Danish expedition to Arctic North America in the charge of the
noted folklorist, Knud Rasmussen. The myths, tales, and legends have
been transcribed in a number of ways: narratives interspersed with
songs and stories recorded in a manner to "put life and substance into
the legends so that in English they read almost as they are apprehended
in Eskimo by one who understands that language as his native tongue";
legends told by the native storyteller prefaced with background material to facilitate the reader's understanding of the literal translation;
and original texts given with an interlinear translation. Information
as to the extent of the folktale material for a particular Eskimo group,
the storyteller's role in his community, and the traditional manner of
telling the tale enhances the importance of the descriptive chapters.

Volumes 7 and 9 are the sources cited in the preface to Knud Rasmussen's *Beyond the High Hills* (Cleveland, World Pub. Co. [1961]
32 p. illus. PM64.Z95E5 1961), a book of Eskimo poetry for children
that includes poems collected among the "Iglulik Eskimos of the Hudson Bay region and the Musk Ox people of the Copper Country."

Some representative titles from this series follow:

31. Birket-Smith, Kaj.
THE CARIBOU ESKIMOS, MATERIAL AND SOCIAL LIFE AND THEIR CUL-
TURAL POSITION. 1929. 2 v. (v. 5)   G670 1921.R25, v. 5
                                                      E99.E7B586

32. Rasmussen, Knud J. V.
INTELLECTUAL CULTURE OF THE HUDSON BAY ESKIMOS. 1930. 3 v.
in 2. (v. 7)   G670 1921.R25, v. 7
                                                      E99.E7R179

33. ———.
THE NETSILIK ESKIMOS, SOCIAL LIFE AND SPIRITUAL CULTURE. 1931.
542 p. (v. 8, no. 1–2)   G670 1921.R25, v. 8, no. 1–2
                                                      E99.E7R194

34. ———.
INTELLECTUAL CULTURE OF THE COPPER ESKIMOS. 1932. 350 p.
(v. 9)   G670 1921.R25, v. 9
                                                      E99.E7R177

35. ———.
THE MACKENZIE ESKIMOS AFTER KNUD RASMUSSEN'S POSTHUMOUS NOTES, edited by H. Ostermann. 1942. 164 p. (v. 10, no. 2)

G670 1921.R25, v. 10, no. 2

36. ———.
THE ALASKAN ESKIMOS AS DESCRIBED IN THE POSTHUMOUS NOTES OF KNUD RASMUSSEN, by H. Ostermann; edited after the latter's death with the assistance of E. Holtved. Translated from the Danish by W. E. Calvert. 1952. 291 p. (v. 10, no. 3)

G670 1921.R25, v. 10, no. 3
E99.E7R15

Children's Editions

37. Bayliss, Clara (Kern).
A TREASURY OF ESKIMO TALES. Illustrated in color by George Carlson. New York, Crowell [c1922] 135 p. col. plates.   E99.E7B2

In the preface the compiler cites as her sources *The Central Eskimo* by Franz Boas (item 24) and *The Eskimo About Bering Strait* by Edward Nelson (item 27). From the lore of the Central Eskimo she has selected 11 stories embellished with the supernatural; they depict ill-treated orphans, strange beings of the sea, and people of extraordinary size and strength. The Bering Strait tales are of Raven the creator—who could push up his beak, making it the visor of a cap, and thus become a man—and how he made man and taught him how to live. In a few tales Raven appears as the victim of his own vanity. The stories are varied, simply retold, with humor and poetic imagination. The subject of "The Giant" straddles an inlet, scooping up whales as other men

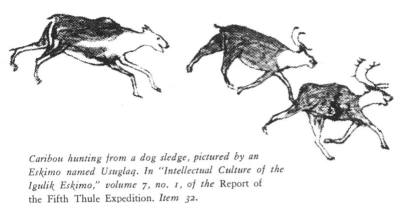

Caribou hunting from a dog sledge, pictured by an Eskimo named Usuglaq. In "Intellectual Culture of the Igulik Eskimo," volume 7, no. 1, of the Report of the Fifth Thule Expedition. *Item 32.*

scoop up minnows; in "Chunks of Daylight" an orphan encounters a man "tossing the snow high in air, and each time he did this the light was hidden, thus causing the changes from light to darkness."

37a. Caswell, Helen R.
  SHADOWS FROM THE SINGING HOUSE; ESKIMO FOLK TALES. Illustrations by Robert Mayokok. Rutland, Vt., C. E. Tuttle Co. [1968]
  108 p.   GR268.E8C3

Eighteen authentic but simplified retellings comprise a collection that is broader in scope than its title indicates, for among the Eskimo stories is a Tsimshian Indian Raven tale, "How the Light Came." In a spare storytelling style well suited to the Eskimo narrative, the author both entertains and conveys a feeling of respect for a remote culture. She provides logical motivation for situations difficult to accept or comprehend—as in the Sedna myth in which the brothers' cruelty is interpreted as an act of fear that is close to madness—and, when necessary to communicate a dramatic moment, introduces background information as an integral part of the story. Her representative selection of Eskimo lore includes tales of monsters and supernatural beings, adventures of hunters and mistreated children, and a few "how and why" stories. The bibliography cites as primary source material Eskimo and Indian texts collected by Franz Boas, Knud Rasmussen, and others. The author is not an ethnologist, but her interest in folklore is described on the jacket as a shared "family interest of 15 years' duration of collecting folk tales from all over the world." She has not followed a formal plan of organization, but in the prologue she discusses three categories of "song"—the form in which the oral heritage was passed on—and comments on the style in which the narrator sings his "song." Soft pencil drawings by an Eskimo artist enhance the attractiveness of the book.

38. Gillham, Charles E.
BEYOND THE CLAPPING MOUNTAINS; ESKIMO STORIES FROM ALASKA.
Illustrations by Chanimun. New York, Macmillan, 1943. 134 p.
E99.E7G44

Thirteen stories about the birds and animals who once lived and acted as real people, told by the Eskimos to entertain one another. The stories were gathered by Mr. Gillham, with the assistance of an English-speaking Eskimo, during the eight summers he spent in Alaska as a biologist for the U.S. Government. In his introduction to these delightfully simple retellings, the compiler states that "the tales are as authentic as it is possible to get them" and that he assumes responsibility for liberties and digressions from the originals. The atmosphere of the bleak and isolated environment of the Eskimo is conveyed by the many details of daily life, as in the tale of the crafty "Mr. Crow" who tries to scare "Miss Mink":

After about half an hour he tiptoed back to the porch door and opened it as quietly as he could. Then he disguised his voice and called out in a low, hollow tone, "I am a ghost, Miss Mink, and I came for the Eskimo ice cream."

Black-and-white line drawings by a young Eskimo girl further enliven the collection.

39. ———.
MEDICINE MEN OF HOOPER BAY; MORE TALES FROM THE CLAPPING MOUNTAINS OF ALASKA. Illustrated by Chanimun. New York, Macmillan [1966? c1955] 134 p.   E99.E7G5

A second collection of Eskimo folklore from Hooper Bay, gathered by the author from "an old Eskimo who had been trained to become a Medicine Man." These are tales of medicine men, or shamans, whose magic was all-powerful, and of orphan children who could see elves, dwarfs, and fairies that were invisible to others. Woven unto these stark, primitive stories, artfully re-created in simple form for children, are short verse-songs, explanatory comments, and fable-like morals. The book is illustrated by the Eskimo artist who, at age 15, illustrated Gillham's earlier collection, *Beyond the Clapping Mountains* (item 38).

40. Keithahn, Edward L.
ALASKAN IGLOO TALES. Illustrated by George A. Ahgupuk. Edited by Kenneth Gilbert. Seattle, R. D. Seal, c1958. 138 p.   E99.E7K39

Earlier title: *Igloo Tales.*

The compiler, in 1923 a teacher in the remote Arctic village of Shismaref, heard these "age-old Eskimo tales" during the long winter nights and recorded them in English "as close to the original Innuit as possible." Here are tales of witchcraft and sorcery, sometimes accounting for Eskimo customs and traditions. Among the titles are "The Boy Who Ate Too Much," "The Robber Dwarfs," and "The Hunter and the Raven." Full-page pencil drawings were made by one of the author's Eskimo schoolboys.

40a. Melzack, Ronald.
THE DAY TUK BECAME A HUNTER & OTHER ESKIMO STORIES. Illustrated by Carol Jones. New York, Dodd, Mead [1967] 92 p.
PZ8.1.M5Day

Ten short tales are retold in a spare style by a Canadian psychologist. His inclusion of the legend of Sedna, goddess of the sea who commands all the sea animals, is a welcome contribution to Eskimo folklore for children. Other stories tell of supernatural encounters of hunters, adventures of orphans, exploits of Raven, and the witch Jatuakju who places toys near the village to entice children to her house. Primary sources are cited for each tale, including the classic works of Franz Boas and Knud Rasmussen and records of other explorers and anthropologists. Handsome two-color woodcuts make this an attractive collection.

"The Woman Who Raised a Bear as Her Son"
sees him off as he goes with the village men to hunt
seal. He wears a seal collar to save him from attack
by hunters from other villages. From The Day Tuk Became
a Hunter & Other Eskimo Stories *by Ronald Melzack;*
woodcuts by Carol Jones. Item 40a.

Detail from Carol Jones' frontispiece to The Day Tuk Became a Hunter & Other Eskimo Stories *by Ronald Melzack. Item 40a.*

41. Rasmussen, Knud J. V., *ed.*
THE EAGLE'S GIFT, ALASKA ESKIMO TALES. Translated by Isobel Hutchinson, illustrated by Ernst Hansen. Garden City, N.Y., Doubleday, Doran, 1932. 235 p., plates, map, col. plates.

E99.E7R173

Authentic Eskimo tales and traditions collected by Mr. Rasmussen during the Fifth Thule Expedition (1921–24), which he led across Arctic America. In transcribing the stories into modern speech he has "striven to spoil nothing of the fine, poetic tone, and the artless vigor which is so characteristic of the primitive spirit and which forms the very pith of the tales." Stories tell of Raven, the creator of all life, and of the remarkable adventures of the hero Wander-Hawk on his quest to avenge the death of his brothers. They are recorded in a manner that makes them suitable for cycle storytelling. The black-and-white line drawings and soft, colored pencil sketches depict details of every-day life and elements of the supernatural. Many of the tales have a stirring, dramatic appeal and enrich an area in which there is little folklore available.

"The Spirit of the Air Helps a Poor Boy," illustrated by
Ernst Hansen, from The Eagle's Gift by Knud Rasmussen.
Item 41.

Mackenzie

Folklore of the Mackenzie area shows a close relation to that of the
Plateau and the North Pacific Coast. Tales from the Wisakedjak cycle
of the Cree are also well known among the Chipewyan. There are no
single editions of Mackenzie folklore for children, but variants of the
tales told in this culture area appear in the collections from neighboring areas. Authentic source material that is broadly representative of
the tribal lore or that includes background discussions of beliefs and
mythology is included in this section.

42. Birket-Smith, Kaj.
CONTRIBUTIONS TO CHIPEWYAN ETHNOLOGY. Copenhagen, Gyldendal, 1930. 113 p. illus. (Report of the 5th Thule expedition 1921–24, v. 6, no. 3)   G670 1921.R25, v. 6, no. 3
    E99.C59B5
Bibliography: p. [111]–113.

In this study of Chipewyan material and intellectual culture are a description of Chipewyan beliefs and mythology and 19 short tales. The background discussion points out the prevalence of stories about animals and how they acquire their various qualities. Among the tales are an amusing account of an argument between Squirrel and Bear as they try to settle upon the length of day and night and a version of the theft of summer. Raven is often the chief tale character.

43. Chapman, John W.
TEN'A TEXTS AND TALES FROM ANVIK, ALASKA. With vocabulary by Pliny E. Goddard. Leyden, E. J. Brill, 1914. 230 p. (Publications of the American Ethnological Society, v. 6)   PM101.A6, v. 6

Contents.—English versions.—Texts.

    A collection of tales from Anvik and the immediate vicinity recorded by John Chapman, whose acquaintance with the Indians of the region began in 1887. The introduction offers general remarks to help the reader better appreciate the character of these stories, the telling of which is one of the Indian's chief recreations. The first group of stories comprises accounts of creation. Mr. Chapman quotes an old Indian who stated, *"The Creator made all things good, but the Raven introduced confusion."* The second group of tales concerns Raven, whose "character is treated with scant respect." In the last group are "the nursery legends and tales evidently invented for the entertainment of children." Commenting on the lack of storytelling appeal that this folklore has for those unacquainted with Indian institutions and "superstitious fancy," the compiler explains, "during the narration, a series of pictures is presented to his [the Indian's] mind which would give point to a tale which to us might seem utterly wanting in interest." Such stories as "Children and Giantess," however, would seem to have universal child appeal.

44. Petitot, Émile F.
TRADITIONS INDIENNES DU CANADA NORD-OUEST. Paris, Maisonneuve Frères et C. Leclerc, 1886. 521 p. (Les littératures populaires de tautes les nations, t. 23)   GR15.L4, v. 23

Contents.—pt. 1. Traditions des Esquimaux Tchiglit.—pt. 2. Traditions des Dindjié ou Loucheux.—pt. 3. Traditions des Dènè Peaux-de-Lièvre.—pt. 4. Traditions des Dunè Flancs-de-chien.—pt. 5. Traditions de Dènè Tchippewayans.—pt. 6. Traditions des Cris.—pt. 7. Traditions des Pieds-Noirs.

Émile Petitot, a Jesuit priest, lived for 20 years in the Canadian Northwest in order to collect the native legends and traditions. He says in his introduction, "Je suis donc le seul ethnographe qui ait conçu le projet de réunir en volume toutes les légendes et traditions nationales du Nord-Ouest du Dominion, partout òu j'ai séjourné ou seulment passé, et qui ait mené ce travail à bonne fin." The 132 legends were recorded with "scrupulous concern for detail" and then literally translated into French with the aid of Indian interpreters. Ethnographic notes introduce each tribal section. The legends are followed by a list of the gods and heroes and an example of the native dialect given in an interlinear translation. Some of the stories are "La création," "L'inondation," "L'homme lunaire," "L'homme sans feu," "Les Hommes-chiens," and "Wisakétchak."

"But every night since that faraway time, Old Man Moon has traveled swiftly through the sky, lighting the earth with his icy stare, endlessly searching for Coyote, who killed his son." Illustration by Dorothy McEntee from Nine Tales of Coyote *by Frances Martin. Item 52.*

Plateau

Coyote, culture hero-trickster and transformer, is the most outstanding actor in Plateau folklore. Of this popular figure Gladys Reichard says, "There are few narratives into which he does not enter either as a primary character or incidentally to put a spoke in somebody's wheel" (item 49). Trickster incidents known among Indian tribes in adjacent culture areas also appear in the Plateau area. The predominance of Coyote tales within this myth body is reflected in the editions for children that follow.

45. Boas, Franz, *ed.*
Folk-tales of Salishan and Sahaptin tribes. New York, American Folklore Society, 1917. 205 p. (Memoirs of the American Folklore Society, v. 11)   GR1.A5, v. 11
                                                          E99.S21B66

Contents.—[pt. 1] Folk-tales of Salishan tribes: 1. Thompson tales, by James A. Teit.—2. Okanagon tales, by James A. Teit.—3. Okanagon tales, by Marian K. Gould.—4. Sanpoil tales, by Marian K. Gould.—5. Pend d'Oreille tales, by James A. Teit.—6. Coeur d'Alene tales, by James A. Teit.—7. Tales from the Lower Fraser River, by James A. Teit.—[pt. 2] Folk-tales of Sahaptin tribes: 8. Sahaptin tales, by Livingston Farrand, edited by Theresa Mayer.—9. Nez Percé tales, by Herbert J. Spinden.

Representative collections are presented with comparative notes by Franz Boas. James Teit recorded background information from Okanagon and Coeur d'Alene narrators. They describe the work of Coyote and Old-One, or Chief, who made the earth and the beings of the "ancient world":

> Now, the Chief said, "If matters are not improved on earth soon, there will be no people." Then he sent Coyote to earth to destroy all the monsters and evil beings, to make life easier and better for the people, and to teach them the best way to do things. . . . Coyote did a great deal of good, but he did not finish everything properly. Sometimes he made mistakes; and although he was wise and powerful, he did many foolish things. He was too fond of playing tricks for his own amusement.

Other stories tell of Fox, Raven, Crow, Owl, Grizzly-Bear, and orphan boys with magical powers. The group of tales associated with the regulation of the seasons and the cold weather is touched with poetry, as in "How the Cold Lost Its Power," which tells of Northern-Lights' five sons—Cold, Colder, Coldest, Extreme-Cold, and Most-Extreme-Cold.

46. Boas, Franz.
Kutenai tales. Together with texts collected by Alexander Chamberlain. Washington, Govt. Print. Off., 1918. 387 p. (Smithsonian Institution. Bureau of American Ethnology. Bulletin 59)
                                                    E51.U6, no. 59
                                                    PM1631.Z73 1918

Original texts collected by Alexander Chamberlain in 1891 are given here in an interlinear and a free translation, and those collected by Dr. Boas in 1914 are given in text and free translation. A final section

discusses the characteristic traits of Kutenai tales: a systematic relationship within the society of animals, and the grouping together of
tales, such as those centering around the creation of the sun or relating
to the war against the sky. The transformer tales of "Ya.ukue'ika.m"
and "Nalmv'qtse." are described as being peculiar to the Kutenai,
whose folktales "show intimate relations to the tales of the tribes of
the plateaus, as well as to those of the plains east of the mountains."
This brief discussion is followed by abstracts and comparative notes.
The tales recorded by Mr. Chamberlain are brief and fragmentary.
Dr. Boas' collection includes versions of tales retold by Frank Linderman (item 51), such as "Rabbit, Coyote, Wolf, and Grizzly Bear,"
"Coyote and the Thunderbirds," "Origin of the Seasons," "Coyote and
Deer," and "Frog and Antelope," but as they appear here they have
little storytelling appeal.

47. Clark, Ella E.
INDIAN LEGENDS FROM THE NORTHERN ROCKIES. Norman, Univer-
sity of Oklahoma Press [1966] 350 p. illus., fold. map, ports. (The
Civilization of the American Indian series)   E78.N77C5

Bibliography: p. 332–344.

This anthology, prepared "for the general reader of any age," includes
myths, legends, personal narratives, and historical traditions. It is a
useful further source of varied and appealing tales. Material was
selected from collections made by ethnologists and from the records
of pioneers, Army officers, missionaries, and others who gathered at
a time when the Indians still knew many of their tribal traditions.
Much of this material, in print for the first time, was taken from
manuscripts in archives and personal collections. The compiler states
as her criteria in editing the "near-literal translation of ethnologists,"
"My ideals of style have been simplicity, sincerity, a conversational
oral quality, and the variety of rhythms in everyday speech." The tales
follow an introductory chapter, "How These Indians Lived," that
characterizes the Plateau and Plains cultures represented in this
anthology.

48. Phinney, Archie.
NEZ PERCÉ TEXTS. New York, Columbia University Press, 1934.
497 p. (Columbia University Contributions to anthropology, v. 25)
                                                    E51.C7, v. 25

"The core of an ancient body of myths which have remained practically intact" were all recorded from a single narrator during the fall
and winter of 1929–30. In his introduction Mr. Phinney refers to "the
striking superiority of this collection from the point of view of native

style, completeness and continuity." Each tale has an interlinear and a free translation; an appendix contains abstracts of some of the stories. These tales are notable for their dialogue and their humor—the "deepest and most vivid element in this mythology"—which Mr. Phinney describes as being droll and ludicrous, with clever exaggerations. Eloise Ramsey notes that Frances Martin's *Nine Tales of Coyote* (item 52) is based considerably upon material found in this book.

49. Reichard, Gladys A.

AN ANALYSIS OF COEUR D'ALENE INDIAN MYTHS. With a comparison by Adele Froelich. Philadelphia, American Folklore Society, 1947 [i.e. 1948] 218 p. (Memoirs of the American Folklore Society, v. 41)   GR1.A5, v. 41

E99.S63R4

"Bibliography and abbreviations": p. 213–216.

Contents.—Introduction.—The style of Coeur d'Alene mythology.—Cultural reflections in Coeur d'Alene mythology.—Diffusion and mythological processes.—The myths and tales.

In a scholarly analysis of the myths and tales of the Coeur d'Alene, a member of the Salish linguistic family, this folklorist examines plots, action, plot motivation, characters and characterization, and stylistic devices. Comparative notes following each tale point out similarities with tales of other Indian groups in the Northwest. Although limited to the Coeur d'Alene, whose mythology is greatly influenced by neighboring Indian lore, this literary analysis increases understanding of the folklore of other North American Indian tribes. Tales of the Coeur d'Alene are also represented in *Folk-Tales of Salishan and Sahaptin Tribes* (item 45).

50. Teit, James A.

TRADITIONS OF THE THOMPSON RIVER INDIANS OF BRITISH COLUMBIA. With introduction by Franz Boas. Boston, For the American Folklore Society by Houghton, Mifflin, 1898. 137 p. (Memoirs of the American Folklore Society, v. 6)   GR1.A5, v. 6

E99.N96T26

For this collection of tales the "prevalent versions" have been selected, with variants given in accompanying notes. Brief abstracts and references to similar tales found among other tribes of North America have been added by Dr. Boas. Important introductory material includes a detailed discussion of the primitive concept of the culture hero and transformer who appears as a great benevolent being, a helper of mankind, and a sly trickster. His actions account for the shaping of the present world. To illustrate this combination of opposite attributes in the figure of the culture hero, examples from the Raven cycle of the Tlingit and Tsimishian Indians and tales of other myth figures such as Glooskap and Manabozho are cited. The folklore of the Thompson River Indians centers on four distinct culture heroes or transformers, the most important of whom is Coyote, the principal character in this series of tales. This collection is useful for background information and as a source of variants.

Children's Editions

51. Linderman, Frank B.
KOOTENAI WHY STORIES, by Frank B. Linderman (Co-skee-see-co-cot) illustrated by Charles L. Bull. New York, Scribner, 1926. 166 p. col. plates.   E99.K85L5

Frank Linderman, who spent many years among the Indians, presents these 15 stories of Nu-la-kin-nah (Old-man) and Skinkoots, the Coyote, as if told by an Indian storyteller. In these simple "how and why" stories, retold in an informal conversational style, the name of the trickster-transformer Nu-la-kin-nah is used interchangeably with Old-man. He is described as having created the world and its inhabitants, "under Ya-cassin-kin-na-waska, the Almighty," and then changing their looks and habits. Mr. Linderman states in his preface that he has "kept as closely to the text as possible, altering no essential points." The stories explain why Skinkoots' arms are thin, how the wicked Co-pee, who traveled about snaring children, was made good, and how the deer lost their sharp teeth.

52. Martin, Frances G. (McEntee).
NINE TALES OF COYOTE. Pictures by Dorothy McEntee. New York, Harper [1950] 60 p.   E98.F6M25

Authentic Nez Percé tales delightfully retold for children. Coyote, who could change himself into animal and human shapes, shows himself variously as the boaster, the clown, the dupe, and the trickster, often falling victim to his own and others' wiles. The smooth narrative with lively dialogue, simple and direct wording, and folk humor make this a very appealing collection. Each of the nine tales opens with a short introduction conveying a sense of time and place and leading directly into the narrative. Bold four-color illustrations suggest the robust action of the stories. According to Eloise Ramsey (item 22) the tales are "faithful in spirit and facts to the sources used" and are based primarily on the collection of *Nez Percé Texts* made by Archie Phinney (item 48), with *Folk Tales of the Salishan and Shahaptin Tribes,* edited by Franz Boas (item 45), "used comparatively."

North Pacific

The tribes of the North Pacific Coast distinguish between two types of stories: myths, which tell of events that happened during the time when animals appeared in the form of human beings; and tales, which are historical in character but contain supernatural elements. Within this large culture area Franz Boas traces the distribution of incidents comprising the Raven cycle from the Asiatic side of the Bering Strait eastward and southward as far as the southern part of Vancouver Island. The names of Raven change from tribe to tribe. The myths about this culture hero, trickster, and transformer recount how he secures fire, sunlight, water, and the other necessities of life for mankind. He then travels about transforming animals and objects until they have their present characteristics. Dr. Boas' detailed comparative study of Tsimshian mythology is still a primary source for compilers and students of folklore. Children's editions offer variety in their selection and arrangement of episodes from the Raven cycle and in their manner of presenting the tales of the totemistic culture heroes.

53. Mourning Dove, *Okinagan Indian.*
    Coyote stories, by Mourning Dove (Humishuma). Edited and
    illustrated by Heister D. Guie, with notes by L. V. McWhorter
    (Old Wolf) and a foreword by Chief Standing Bear. Caldwell,
    Idaho, Caxton Printers, 1933. 228 p. illus., plates, port.
    PZ8.1.M867Co
    Illustrated lining-papers.

Mourning Dove states in her preface that old storytellers who traveled
from village to village told these stories to amuse the children. Background information and explanations of Indian customs are given in
footnotes. In these tales Spirit Chief gives Coyote the responsibility of
making the world ready for man and of ridding the world of "People-
Devouring Monsters." But more often he appears as the trickster, getting into mischief and stirring up trouble. Magic and the ability to
restore life play a large part in furthering the action. The stories are
authentically told, without embellishments or interpolations, by an
editor who did not attempt to translate the colorful narrative style of
the Indian storyteller described by Mourning Dove.

54. Boas, Franz, *ed.*
    Bella Bella tales. New York, American Folklore Society, G. E.
    Stechert, agents, 1932. 178 p. (Memoirs of the American Folklore
    Society, v. 25) GR1.A5, v. 25

The material in this collection was gathered by Dr. Boas in the fall of
1923. He writes that the "tales of the Bella Bella embody most of the
elements characteristic of the North Pacific Coast mythologies and
folktales." He portrays briefly the traits that characterize the tales
of this area, in contrast to other areas, and the growth of Indian
mythologies. Some of the selections are grouped as follows: "The
Raven Tales," "Mink [Stories]," "Ancestor Tales," "Tales of Deserted
Children," "Novelistic Tales," and "Tales of Encounters With Supernatural Beings." Comparative footnotes have been added. Of particular interest is the version of the "Cannibal-of-the-North-End-of-the-
World," which has been retold in editions for children.

55. Boas, Franz.
    Kwakiutl tales, new series. New York, Columbia University
    Press, 1935–43. 2 v. (Columbia University contributions to anthro-
    pology, v. 26 [pt. 1–2]) E51.C7, v. 26, pt. 1–2

Contents.—1. Translation.—2. Texts.
These tales were collected by Dr. Boas during the winter of 1930–31

and are given in an English translation described in the preface as "quite literal." Trickster and transformer tales are prominent; others concern ghosts and dwarfs. Historical tales are numerous. Comparative notes bring together Kwakiutl versions contained in various publications and also cite the comparative discussion of Tsimshian mythology in the 31st *Annual Report of the U.S. Bureau of American Ethnology* (item 56).

56. ———.

TSIMSHIAN MYTHOLOGY. Based on texts recorded by Henry W. Tate. *In* U.S. *Bureau of American Ethnology*. Annual report. 31st; 1909/10. Washington, 1916. p. 29–1037. illus., plates.

E51.U55 31st

Bibliography: p. 39–41.

A collection of myths identified by Franz Boas as "the bulk of the important traditions of the Tsimshian." Included are 38 individual Raven myths and 66 other tales; a "Description of the Tsimshian, Based on Their Mythology"; a "Comparative Study of Tsimshian Mythology"; and appendixes that contain a few "Bellabella and Nootka Tales" and a detailed "Index to References" cited in the comparative study.

Dr. Boas' analysis of the character of the culture heroes of the North Pacific Coast and his description of tale differences among the various tribes offer a clearer insight into this lore.

This collection has been a primary source for folklorists who have retold stories from the Raven cycle for children. The narrative style is illustrated in this example from the "Origin of Daylight":

The whole world was still covered with darkness. When the sky was clear, the people would have a little light from the stars; and when clouds were in the sky, it was very dark all over the land. The people were distressed by this. Then Giant [Raven] thought that it would be hard for him to obtain his food if it were always dark. He remembered that there was light in heaven, whence he had come. Then he made up his mind to bring down the light to our world.

57. Jacobs, Melville.

THE CONTENT AND STYLE OF AN ORAL LITERATURE; CLACKAMAS CHINOOK MYTHS AND TALES. New York, Wenner-Gren Foundation for Anthropological Research, 1959. 285 p. (Viking Fund publications in anthropology, no. 26) E99.C818J3 1959a

Bibliographical references included in "Notes" (p. 273).

Contents.—pt. 1. Analyses of eight stories.—pt. 2. The literature as a whole.—pt. 2A. Features of content.—pt. 2B. Features of style.

A specialized study of the oral literature of a now virtually extinct

people of the Pacific Northwest. Dr. Jacobs illustrates with examples
his method of presenting an oral literature "to supplement the bare
dictations which dominate the archives of folklore." He explains the
difficulty of comprehending and appreciating the oral literature of a
primitive people: "Narrators usually delivered relatively bare bones of
their stories, while the native audience immediately filled in with
many associations and feelings which a non-member of the group
could not possibly have." The method used in this study shows a way
of "placing flesh upon the bones of translated dictations."

A "sociocultural" sketch of the people provides background for the
lore. The eight stories in part 1 are presented first as they were dictated and then in a freer version woven into the interpretation. The
detailed comparative analysis of content and style in part 2 considers
the characteristic features of this literature—for example, personalities,
humor, stylized devices, and motifs.

58. ———.
   Coos MYTH TEXTS. Seattle, University of Washington, 1940. p. 129–
   259. (University of Washington publications in anthropology, v. 8,
   no. 2, Apr. 1940)   PM1611.Z73J17, v. 8

Most of these texts were gathered from a single narrator during the
summers of 1933 and 1934. Melville Jacobs claims they are frank and
unexpurgated. The narrator, he says, "has also given these myths in
what I think may be a stylistic cloak that is akin to the best traditions
of the ancient art of myth telling among the Coos." For background
relating to the collection of these texts and discussion of their stylistic
devices the reader is referred to the compiler's other published monographs and papers. Mention is made only of the conventional closing
of a folktale, or myth, which forecasts what an animal's future behavior
will be when Indians have settled the land. Among the tales are those
of tricksters, including Coyote, and Bluejay. All are given in the original Indian dialect and English translation. A final section of abstracts
incorporates "all Coos stories that Coos field workers have obtained."

59. ———.
   KALAPUYA TEXTS. Seattle, University of Washington, 1945. 394 p.
   illus. (map) (University of Washington publications in anthropology, v. 11, June 1945)   PM1421.Z73J3, v. 11

Original texts with English translations.

Contents.—pt. 1. Santiam Kalapuya ethnologic texts, by Melville
Jacobs.—pt. 2. Santiam Kalapuya myth texts, by Melville Jacobs.—
pt. 3. Kalapuya texts, by Albert S. Gatschet, Leo J. Frachtenberg, and
Melville Jacobs.

Dr. Jacobs pictures his researches, carried on in a number of brief sessions between 1928 and 1936, as a "last-hour salvage job." Following the preface, in which he discusses the native style of speech, he presents 92 ethnologic texts describing Indian traditions. Nineteen myths following in part 2 represent "a small segment of the old Santiam Kalapuya mythology" and were narrated in a "fairly genuine Santiam literary style." The 49 items in part 3 include both ethnologic texts and myths. In a final section are abstracts of all the known Kalapuya myths and tales and an index of ethnographic items noted in the ethnographic and folkloristic texts in this volume.

Coyote appears as the principal tale character in this series of myths.

60. Jacobs, Melville, *ed.*
    NORTHWEST SAHAPTIN TEXTS. v. 1. Seattle, University of Washington Press, 1929. [244] p. ports. (University of Washington publications in anthropology, v. 2, no. 6)   PM2301.Z73J3 1929

The significance of this collection is stated by the compiler: "The texts in Sahaptin, of which this represents a fraction, were collected in the course of a number of trips made with linguistic purposes in mind; the texts were obtained from many informants and translated by several interpreters. In the notes I endeavour to present a picture of the conditions under which the texts were gathered; I especially attempt to describe the informant and interpreter."

The tales are variously transcribed here in interlinear translations, in the native Indian dialect, and in "free English translations." Some of the characters represented here are Coyote, Timber Rabbit, Wild Cat, Beaver, and Flying Squirrel.

61. Jacobs, Melville.
    NORTHWEST SAHAPTIN TEXTS. New York, Columbia University Press, 1934–37. 2 v. (Columbia University contributions to anthropology, v. 19, pt. 1–2)   E51.C7, v. 19, pt. 1–2

"Additional" myths and miscellaneous texts from the Klickitat and adjacent Sahaptin tribes (Cowlitz and Upper Cowlitz) and two Kittitas myths, collected at various times from 1926 to 1930. In his preface the compiler states, "Very little of the atmosphere of story telling can be provided on a printed page." The dictations of each informant are grouped together and are preceded by short descriptive and critical notes about the informant and interpreter. These comments indicate that some of the dictations are "fragmentary in content and fail in proper use of native myth narrative style" or that they were recorded "to satisfy linguistic curiosity." Coyote appears as the main character. Abstracts are given in a final section.

62. Swanton, John R.
    TLINGIT MYTHS AND TEXTS. Washington, Govt. Print. Off., 1909.
    451 p. (Smithsonian Institution. Bureau of American Ethnology.
    Bulletin 39)   E51.U6, No. 39   PM2455.Z73S8 1909
                          E99.T6S97   E99.T6S972

Issued also as House Document 1528, U.S. 60th Congress, 2d session.

Myths and texts collected at Sitka and Wrangell, Alaska, in 1904. The
myths are given in literal English translations. The texts appear both
in their original language with an interlinear translation and in literal
English translations. Brief introductions to the stories name the individual narrators. Mr. Swanton identifies the narrative style of Dekina'k!
of Sitka as "entirely after the ancient patterns." Background information is limited to footnotes explaining obscure passages or references
to other published collections. Raven episodes recorded both at Sitka
and Wrangell are brief, with little detail. Other tales that appear in
editions for children depict the little otters who looked like human
beings from the waist up. Abstracts of the myths follow in a concluding section.

Children's Editions

63. Ayre, Robert.
    SKETCO, THE RAVEN. Illustrated by Philip Surrey. Toronto, Mac-
    millan [1967, ᶜ1961] 183 p.   PZ8.1.A9Sk4

American edition (New York, St. Martin's Press, 1962).

Fourteen tales drawn from the Raven cycle, common to the Indians
along the northern Pacific Coast. "While I have used my imagination
in re-creating the Raven tales," states Mr. Ayre, "I have endeavoured
to be true to the life and character of the people who told them and,
confident in the authenticity of my version, I pay my respects to the
ethnologists who collected them from the Indians, with particular
gratitude to Franz Boas, James A. Teit, Diamond Jenness and Marius
Barbeau."
    The first episodes describe how Sketco steals the stars, moon, and
sun from the Great Chief, Nass-shig-ee-yatlth, who would "pore over
them as misers pore over their riches." In the remaining adventures
Raven sets out to bring his brothers back from the land of the dead

and to punish his wicked uncle. In his travels he visits the bottom of the ocean and is held captive by Thunder and Lightning. Raven is arrogant and boastful and will trick by flattery, but he has a good heart. The personalities of the characters have been fully developed, and the action is described in lively detail. Vivid ink drawings illustrate the stories.

64. Grinnell, George B.
THE PUNISHMENT OF THE STINGY, AND OTHER INDIAN STORIES. New York, Harper, 1901. 234 p. col. front. (port.), plates. (Harper's portrait collection of short stories, v. 5)   PZ3.G8934P, v. 5

"Seated by the flickering fire in Blackfoot skin-lodge, or in Pawnee dirt-house, or in sea-shore dwelling on the northwest coast, I have received these stories from the lips of aged historians, and have set them down here as I have heard them." Thus the famous collector-teller introduces 16 tales that he knows must be "reproduced as they are told; otherwise they lose that primitive flavor which is often one of their chief charms."

The three Bluejay stories—"The Punishment of the Stingy," "Bluejay, the Imitator," and "Bluejay Visits the Ghosts"—with their eerie atmosphere and touches of humor give the collection special appeal. Also of marked interest is "The Blindness of Pi-wap-ok," a moving Northwest tale of courage rewarded by a bird's gift of secret power so that a blind warrior becomes a great medicine man and healer of the sick. "The Beaver Stick" is another tale of magic powers granted, in which a poor, ragged orphan proves himself and wins the girl who understands that all he needs to change his ways are kindness and teaching.

65. Harris, Christie.
ONCE UPON A TOTEM. Woodcuts by John F. Mills. New York, Atheneum, 1963. 148 p.   E98.F6H29

From the home of the Haida, Tsimshian, Tlingit, and Kwakiutl—the North Pacific coastland from Alaska to Oregon—come these four legends and an account of a historical incident. In her retellings Mrs. Harris, a native of British Columbia, has drawn upon the legendary history of mythical heroes symbolized on the totem poles characteristic of this area: Thunderbird, Wolf, Killer-Whale, Raven, and Grizzly Bear. The stories are based on ethnological reports and the author's direct contact with the Indians.

A critical appraisal of this collection by Sheila Egoff, a Canadian professor of children's literature, applauded it for sheer narrative power and the successful weaving of authentic background material into the stories, giving them a uniquely Indian character. "The potential for children's literature inherent in the Indian legends," Miss Egoff writes, "is most fully realized by Christie Harris in *Once Upon a Totem* (1963). Other collections have, perhaps, more charm, or a more fluid style, but the legends chosen by Mrs. Harris and her interpretation of them are outstanding in that they seek quietly to illuminate universal values. The stories are very much a part of early Indian life and very much a part of today" (*In Review, Canadian Books for Children,* winter 1967: 8–9).

Striking woodcuts are based on the art of the Pacific Northwest.

66. Hillyer, William H.
THE BOX OF DAYLIGHT. With drawings by Erick Berry. New York, Knopf, 1931. 179 p. PZ8.1.H559Bo

Woodcut of wise Raven, who leads a spirit boy to the home of the "Wild Woman of the Woods," to rescue village children from being smoked like fish for the giantess' next meal. From Once Upon a Totem *by Christie Harris; woodcuts by John Frazer Mills. Item 65.*

Illustrations by Dorothy McEntee from Nine Tales of Raven *by Frances Martin*

include this one for "Eagle Boy," printed in brown, black, and green. Item 67.

A volume of 33 short, easy-to-read stories in a hero cycle about Tchamsem the Raven, based on tales gathered from the Haida, Tlingit, and Tsimshian tribes by Dr. Franz Boas, whose ethnological study was contained in the 31st *Annual Report of the U.S. Bureau of American Ethnology* (item 56). Offering the essentials of the myths from the "contradictory versions" contained in the report, Mr. Hillyer in his simple narration retains the somber dignity of the Indian's style. He considers this lore to be "one of the most fascinating and colorful of the legends of North America"—a story of creation with a "real hero, Indian style . . . brave, strong, boastful, crafty, devoted, greedy, treacherous." "Tchamsem is Born" opens as follows:

Here begins the most amazing part of the whole history of Raven; wherein we see him outwitting celestial beings, triumphing over obstacles—almost defying the decrees of the supernatural gods; which had he not done, we should have had no daylight, no fire, no fresh water, no halibut, no salmon; indeed, it is doubtful if we ourselves should have existed, you and I.

Erick Berry has made effective use of Indian designs for chapter-head decorations and other illustrations.

67. Martin, Frances G. (McEntee).
    NINE TALES OF RAVEN. Pictures by Dorothy McEntee. New York, Harper [1951] 60 p.   E98.F6M26

Nine tales based on the myths of the Tsimshian, Bellabella, Kwakiutl, and Tlingit Indians. In her acknowledgments Mrs. Martin notes that since "the incidents of one story were often met again in a quite different setting and involving quite different characters, the author has felt free to make new combinations of her own." She cites as her sources *Tsimshian Mythology, Bella Bella Tales, and Kwakiutl Tales*, by Franz Boas (items 56, 54, and 55, respectively), and *Tlingit Myths and Texts*, by John R. Swanton (item 62).

The two sides of Raven's character are represented in this varied selection: "Raven Who Sets Things Right" and "The Greedy One." An economy of words and conversation and the familiar folktale elements of cumulative pattern and magical devices add to the appeal of these retellings. The illustrations were done "after the closest study of all the available Northwest Coast Indian art."

68. Running, Corinne.
    WHEN COYOTE WALKED THE EARTH; INDIAN TALES OF THE PACIFIC NORTHWEST. Illustrated by Richard Bennett. New York, Henry Holt [1949] 71 p.   E98.F6R8

Fourteen Coyote myths from the time when only animals lived on earth—when they talked like men, but acted like animals—selected for children and reworked to make them "more suitable" and "intelligible." The author culled them from Melville Jacobs' earlier translations of the folklore of the Indians of Oregon and Washington; some stories are still told by Indians in the State of Washington. Mr. Jacobs praised the author for being "sensitively appreciative of those qualities in the esoteric oral literatures which make them entertaining to non-Indian young people. . . . Translation into English of course involved . . . the loss of stylistic features which are many and complex in the Indians' recitations of myths in their native languages and cultural settings."

Illustrator Richard Bennett's wintry scene for "How Spring Came" from When Coyote Walked the Earth *by Corinne Running. Item 68.*

California

A diverse selection of tales from the California Indians has been retold for children. Among them are variant accounts of the creation, from the northwestern, central, and southern areas, and versions of the theft of fire, light, and the sun. Many tales concern the transformation of the world into its present shape; some have to do with physiographic features; others are simple etiological narratives. Coyote appears as the outstanding tale character and is presented in various, often anti-thetical, roles. These have been summed up by Samuel Barrett (item 69): an actual creator, or an assistant who in part cooperates and in part thwarts the true creator; a beneficent culture hero or a malevolent being; an allwise powerful shaman or a credulous fool; and a crafty trickster or the butt of ridicule.

69. Barrett, Samuel A., *ed.*
    POMO MYTHS. Milwaukee, Published by Order of the Board of
    Trustees [1933] 608 p. (Bulletin of the Public Museum of the
    City of Milwaukee, v. 15, Nov. 6, 1933)   QH1.M63, v. 15
                                                     E99.P65B25
Bibliography: p. 549–553.

An extensive collection of myths representative of the lore of the Pomo
tribes of central California. These myths were gathered in 1914 and
1915 from the older Indians to whom tribal customs and beliefs were
still meaningful. A significant part of this work is the background
information supplied by the compiler: a summary of the characteristics
of Pomo mythology, descriptions of the mythical characters, a comparative study of Pomo mythology with that of other tribes of the
central California area, abstracts, analytical notes, and a motif index.

Both the detailed versions and the story fragments are given in
"free translations" in "the full Indian form, with its many repetitions,"
and each narrative is presented as a long continued story, incident following incident at great length, according to the style of the individual
informant. The variants show considerable difference in detail and
sequence of incidents. The principal subjects concern the "Bird-people,"
including mammals—the supernatural beings that inhabited the earth
before the creation of the present race of human beings—and the
transformation of the world to its present condition. Coyote appears
as the most important character and plays the role of the culture hero,
transformer, and trickster.

Stories in this collection that have been retold for children include
"Sapsucker Tricks Coyote in Hair-dressing" and "The Rescue From
Growing Rock by Measuring Worm."

70. Curtin, Jeremiah.
    MYTHS OF THE MODOCS. Boston, Little, Brown, 1912. 389 p.
                                                     E99.M7C9

Fifty-nine stories, many of them long, episodic narratives without
clear motivation, were related to Jeremiah Curtin in 1884 by two of
the tribe's oldest members. Background information is limited to a
section of interpretive notes. No arrangement is followed in presenting the tales. Kumush the creator, Sun, Moon, and other forces of
nature, as well as familiar animals, are frequent tale personages.

Mr. Curtin recorded a version of the capture of Witsduk, "Snow
That the Wind Blows and Drifts," a story that also appears in folktale
collections for children.

71. Gifford, Edward W., *and* Gwendoline H. Block, *comps.*
CALIFORNIA INDIAN NIGHTS ENTERTAINMENTS; STORIES OF THE CREA-
TION OF THE WORLD, OF MAN, OF FIRE, OF THE SUN, OF THUNDER,
ETC.; OF COYOTE, THE LAND OF THE DEAD, THE SKY LAND, MONSTERS,
ANIMAL PEOPLE, ETC. Glendale, Calif., Arthur H. Clark Co., 1930.
323 p. fold. map, plates. E98.R3G45

Eighty-two myths and tales from the principal regions of California,
selected by two ethnologists, have been "adapted" from those recorded
and published by anthropologists in the *Journal of American Folklore*
and the publications of the University of California and the American
Museum of Natural History. Introductory material describes the
northwestern, central, and southern cultures and the linguistic diver-
sity of the California Indian tribes. Under the heading "Story Telling"
are discussions of the traditions associated with this art, the manner
of telling, and the types of stories. Also considered are the popular
episodes in California mythology and the individual tale characters.
Dialogue enlivens the simple narrative style of this collection.

72. Kroeber, Alfred L.
HANDBOOK OF THE INDIANS OF CALIFORNIA. Washington, Govt.
Print. Off., 1925. 995 p. illus., 83 plates on 49 l. (incl. maps, part
fold.) (Smithsonian Institution. Bureau of American Ethnology.
Bulletin 78) E51.U6, no. 78

Bibliography: p. 943–966.

Detailed descriptions of the intellectual and material culture and social
organization of 50 California tribes, to which are added comparative
discussions, comprise this compendium. The compiler has gathered
together material never before printed, some of it based on his own
research, and material made available by members of the Department
of Anthropology of the University of California. The selective bibliography has brief appraisals of many of the titles listed. Sections on
tribal mythology comment on the literary style and describe the culture heroes, tricksters, and supernatural beings such as the following:
"The grandeur of the concept of our earth as a vast horned animal
that wallows southward through the primeval waters with Nagaicho
standing on its head, until it comes to rest lying down in its present
position, can not be denied."

73. Kroeber, Theodora.
THE INLAND WHALE. Foreword by Oliver La Farge. Drawings by
Joseph Crivy. Bloomington, Indiana University Press [1959] 205 p.
E98.F6K82
Includes bibliography: p. 203–205.

A collection for adults of nine varied and absorbing stories retold with a "sense of poetry and drama" from the folklore and mythology of the California Indian. Commentaries in a concluding section may give the reader an appreciation and understanding of unedited texts, since each discusses the culture and values of the tribe from which the story was collected, the literary aspects of the tale, and something of its history. The foreword by Oliver La Farge, in which he refers to this collection as "truly impressive" literature "in the best sense of the word," and the author's introduction indicate problems encountered in the selection and retelling of these primitive tales.

74. Latta, Frank F.
CALIFORNIA INDIAN FOLKLORE, as told to F. F. Latta, by Wah-nom'-kot, Wah-hum'-chah, Lee'-mee [and others] Shafter, Calif., 1936. 209 p. plates, ports.   E98.F6L34

Thirty-two myths and tales, most of which are from the Yokuts of central California and a few from the neighboring Miwok, are told simply and without literary elaboration. They were gathered by the editor, who worked for many years among the few remaining tribesmen. The tales are grouped according to subject: "Creation Stories," "Fire Stealing Stories," "Origin Stories," "Mythical Games," "Stories of Yosemite," "Stories of the Heavens," "Mythical Hero Stories," and "Creation of Man." Brief background notes and a list of characters precede each story, some of which are related in a number of versions. In each of the four accounts of the theft of fire a different bird or animal is the hero.

75. Merriam, Clinton H., ed.
THE DAWN OF THE WORLD; MYTHS AND WEIRD TALES TOLD BY THE MEWAN INDIANS OF CALIFORNIA. Cleveland, Arthur H. Clark Co., 1910. 273 p. plates (part col.), map.   E99.M69M5

"Bibliography of California mythology": p. 243–246.

The tales and beliefs of the Miwok tribes of central California. In editing these story "fragments," the compiler, an anthropologist and naturalist, states that his "aim has been to reproduce them in simple English, adhering as closely as possible to the forms in which they were told me by the Indians." Background material offers the reader a viewpoint necessary for the full appreciation and enjoyment of the tales and summarizes the "Fundamental Elements of Mewan Mythology" and the "Characteristics of the FIRST PEOPLE Perpetuated in Their Final Forms." Each tale is preceded by a list of the mythical characters and a statement of the locality or group from which it was secured. Summaries of variants occasionally follow the tales. The collection is

arranged in two parts, "Ancient Myths" and "Present Day Myths." In part 1 are the adventures of the "FIRST PEOPLE"—beings who inhabited the country for a long period before man was created—the creation of the Indian people by Coyote-man, and the transformation of the "FIRST PEOPLE" into animals and other objects of nature. The beliefs described in part 2 relate to animals, ghosts, death, natural phenomena, witches, pigmies, giants, and other fabulous beings.

76. Powers, Stephen.
TRIBES OF CALIFORNIA. Washington, Govt. Print. Off., 1877. 635 p. illus., fold. map, plan. (Contributions to North American ethnology, v. 3)   E71.C76, v. 3

At head of title: Department of the Interior. U.S. Geographical and Geological survey of the Rocky Mountain region. J. W. Powell, in charge.

Information about the habits, customs, legends, religious beliefs, and geographical distribution of the California Indians was gathered by the compiler during 3 years of residence and travel among these tribes. The myths and legends are only a small part of this lengthy, detailed study. The four "Karok Fables" told by the women to amuse the children are compared in interest to the fables of Aesop. One of these short "how and why" stories is a fresh version of "The Coyotes Dancing With the Stars," which accounts for the existence of meteors. In a humorous Miwok version of the "Creation of Man" all the animals are eager to contribute some quality of which they are very proud, such as "a mighty voice," or "a magnificent pair of antlers."

In his preface to the *Handbook of the Indians of California* (item 72) Alfred Kroeber says of Powers' "classic" work: "Anthropologically his great service lies in the fact that with all the looseness of his data and method he was able to a greater degree than any one before or after him to seize and fix the salient qualities of the mentality of the people he described."

Children's Editions

77. CURRY, JANE L.
DOWN FROM THE LONELY MOUNTAIN; CALIFORNIA INDIAN TALES. Illustrated by Enrico Arno. New York, Harcourt, Brace & World [1965] 128 p.   E78.C15C8

Coyote begs to learn "Cottontail's Song," in Down From the Lonely Mountain *by Jane Louise Curry; illustrator, Enrico Arno. Item 77.*

Wives and spouses in "What Happened to Six Wives Who Ate Onions," from Stories California Indians Told *by Anne Fisher. Ruth Robbins, illustrator. Item 78.*

Retellings of 12 tales set in the time when the world was new and the animals helped to shape it. According to the book jacket, the compiler, a college teacher of English and a storyteller, drew upon her own background of California Indian lore and her research at the British Museum. "Where some [tales] were fragmentary, she filled in gaps with similar situations found in other California Indian tales."

Among the animal characters are Coyote, Wus the Fox, Mouse, Cottontail, Blue Jay, and Kaai the Crow. Other myth figures are the Wind People, Thunder and his daughters Churning Cloud, Heavy Rain, Storm Ice, and Swift-as-Lightning, and the old medicine woman Witsduk or "Snow the Wind Blows and Drifts." Some episodes portray the theft of the sun, moon, dawn, and fire; many others explain how the world and the animals living today acquired their present characteristics. In one humorous tale Coyote tries to learn Cottontail's song. To build the stories anew, Miss Curry has enlarged upon motivation and injected subtle humor. Pen and ink drawings depict the animal characters.

78. Fisher, Anne (Benson).
   STORIES CALIFORNIA INDIANS TOLD. Illustrated by Ruth Robbins.
   Berkeley, Calif., Parnassus Press [1957] 109 p.   E98.F6F5

The foreword by an associate professor of anthropology at San Francisco State College affirms, "The California Indian stories in this book are authentic. Most of the myths were collected by the famous early anthropologist and naturalist Dr. C. Hart Merriam who wrote the tales down just as they were told to him by Indian story-tellers. Dr. Merriam then related the myths to the author who turned them into stories for children and young people."

These 12 tales represent the lore of the three main, culturally distinct regions of California. The seven tribes identified in the individual stories are the Gabrielino, Pomo, Yokuts, Karok, Mono, Achomawi, and Miwok. A simple narrative style recounts events in the early days of the world, such as how the Great Spirit made California on the backs of the Turtle Brothers, how Coyote and Eagle helped to light the world, and how Old-Man-Above made Mt. Shasta. In all the tales the animals think like human beings, exert almost unlimited physical powers, and act with ingenuity, bravery, and daring. Lively three-color illustrations depict the animal and Indian characters.

Plains

Collections of Plains Indian stories reveal the notable popularity of two tale types: that of the trickster, and that relating to sacred origins. Together they reflect the Indian's love of fun, reverence for nature, and belief in spiritual forces.

Sacred stories offer an explanation of esoteric ceremonies and/or account for their origin, and describe the experiences of those who secure medicine power or a guardian spirit. Some of these tales became the private property of the priesthood or religious organizations, and some the property of individuals. Gradually these myths found their way among ordinary people, becoming common property, and, in being told merely for entertainment, lost much of their original meaning and religious significance. This would account in part for the number of variants available. The dramatic fulfillment provided by tales in this group is effected by the relationship of myth to ritual, depending on whether a story's climax comes simply with the transfer of medicine power or whether the tale has its own culminating incident.

Trickster tales, usually pointing up a moral, were told for entertainment. Among the Plains tribes, variations on the trickster's name are frequent. He appears as Old Man or Na'pi (Blackfeet), Wihio (Cheyenne), Saynday or Sen'deh (Kiowa), Wesukechak (Northern Manitoba Swampy Cree), Unktomee (Sioux), and Coyote (Skidi Pawnee). Stith Thompson, in *The Folktale* (item 9), characterizes the trickster's adventures as a succession of clever tricks and foolish mishaps as he alternately plays the role of beneficent culture hero, clever deceiver, or numskull.

79. Dorsey, George A.
    THE CHEYENNE. Chicago, 1905. 178 p. illus. (part. col.), plates, maps, plans, diagrs. (Field Columbian Museum. Publication 99, 103. Anthropological series, v. 9, no. 1–2) GN2.F4, v. 9, no. 1–2
                                                                  E99.C53D7
                                                          E51.F45, v. 9, no. 1–2
A detailed description of the Medicine-Arrow Ceremony, the Medicine Dance (or Sun Dance), and five warrior societies is accompanied here by four myths accounting for the origin of these societies and ceremonies. The tales appear "with but slight changes, as they were obtained through Richard Davis, a full-blood Cheyenne." "The Origin of the Medicine-Arrows," especially, has dramatic interest and a strong storytelling appeal in its fullness of plot, its clear, straightforward style, and details of magical transformations. It tells how Standing-Medicine or Standing Sweet-Grass (Motzeyouf), who slew a wicked chief, fled to his grandmother's lodge and made his escape in vapor arising from an overturned vessel. Later he returned to his people with the medicine-arrows. The description of the ceremonies reenacting the original transfer of medicine power to a human owner (also accounted for in the origin myths) makes clear the significance of these myths, which are often obscure and meaningless when presented out of their cultural context.

80. ———.
    TRADITIONS OF THE SKIDI PAWNEE. With introduction notes, and illustrations. Boston, For the American Folklore Society by Houghton, Mifflin, 1904. 366 p. plates, ports. (Memoirs of the American Folklore Society, v. 8) GR1.A5, v. 8
                                                                  E99.P3D7
An extensive collection of Pawnee tales, some of which have not been retold in collections for children, are grouped as "Cosmogonic," "Boy Heroes," "Medicine," "Animal Tales," "People Marry Animals or Become Animals," and "Miscellaneous." In the introduction the author discusses the Pawnee religion, the Pawnee's pantheon, and his explanation of the medicine bundles—their significance and ownership rights, associated ceremonies, dances, and tales of origin. Mr. Dorsey makes meaningful a type of tale widely distributed throughout this culture area. He also includes abstracts of the tales, explanatory and comparative notes, and a bibliography of the sources quoted.
    In a moving narrative, "Lightning Visits the Earth," the storyteller will find a pleasing sonority of language and richness of imagery. "Turtle's War-Party" and "Fox and Rabbit" parallel familiar Brer

Rabbit stories while at the same time introducing magical transformations that give them a unique Indian flavor. "Speak-Riddles and Wise-Spirit," a tale of unusual charm, attempts to answer an insoluble riddle concerning one man's imaginative observation of the world around him.

81. Grinnell, George B.
BLACKFOOT LODGE TALES; THE STORY OF A PRAIRIE PEOPLE. Lincoln, University of Nebraska Press, 1962. 310 p. illus. (A Bison book, BB 129)   E99.S54G83 1962

A reissue in paperback of Grinnell's classic work, first published by Scribner in 1892. This collection of tales, from the prairie people who form a part of the western outlying branch of the great Algonquian linguistic stock, offers a rewarding source of storytelling material. Mr. Grinnell lived and hunted with these Indians and recorded stories told by their old men and warriors. He presents them in the words of their original narrators "as nearly as it is possible to render those words into the simplest every-day English." His style is heroic and dramatic, touched with poetry and romance without being sentimental.

The tales fall into four categories: stories of warriors' adventures; incidents of camp life, hunting, and war excursions; tales of the origin of rituals and of magical transformations; and accounts of Old Man, told solely for entertainment. The stories of ritual origins include full descriptions of the rituals. In the last group of stories, the character of Old Man, who is conceived of as a flesh-and-blood person, reveals a "curious mixture of opposite attributes."

In a final section Mr. Grinnell discusses the history, customs, and mythology of the Blackfeet.

82. ———.
BY CHEYENNE CAMPFIRES. With photographs by Elizabeth C. Grinnell. New Haven, Yale University Press [1962] 305 p. (A Yale Western Americana paperbound, YW–2)
                                                                E99.C53G76 1962

These myths, folktales, and historical narratives, first published in 1926, were gathered over a period of 40 years dating from the author's first contact with this Plains tribe in 1890. Grinnell recorded the stories in approximately the form in which they were told "during winter months in a Cheyenne teepee." In his introduction, "The Cheyenne and Their Stories," he describes the oral literature of the Cheyenne as extensive and varied, with some very old tales and others dealing with matters of "but a generation or two ago." He includes "War Stories," "Stories of Mystery," "Hero Myths," "The Earliest Stories," "Culture

Hero Stories" (including tales about Standing on the Ground and
Sweet Medicine), and "Wihio" (a trickster) stories. This selection,
representative of the range of Cheyenne mythology, is broader than
that appearing in any collection for children. However, as a source for
storytelling it lacks the appeal of the *Blackfoot Lodge Tales; the Story
of a Prairie People* (item 81).

*An episode from the myth of the origin of the Sun Dance, by a Cheyenne artist,
from* The Cheyenne *by George A. Dorsey. The medicine man, attired in his
horned cap, and his chosen woman leave the holy mountain, where they have
received ceremonial instruction from the Great Medicine and the Roaring
Thunder. A great herd of buffalo appears and follows them back to their people,
who are suffering from famine. Item 79.*

83. ———.

PAWNEE HERO STORIES AND FOLK-TALES; WITH NOTES ON THE ORIGIN,
CUSTOMS, AND CHARACTER OF THE PAWNEE PEOPLE. Introduction by
Maurice Frink. Lincoln, University of Nebraska Press, 1961. 417 p.
illus. (A Bison book, BB 116)   E99.P3G8 1961

"The text of this book is reproduced from the edition published in
1889 by the Forest and Stream Publishing Company, New York."

Two Grinnell collections, this one and *Blackfoot Lodge Tales; the
Story of a Prairie People* (item 81), "are among the classic contributions to the folklore of the American Indian" (item 22). *Pawnee Hero
Stories and Folk-Tales* covers mythological and historical Pawnee
heroes and the "miraculous doings of the olden time." These stories
were told to Mr. Grinnell by the Indians and literally translated into
simple English with no attempt at giving them "literary color." In
contrast to *Blackfoot Lodge Tales,* this collection is valuable for the
picture it gives of the Pawnee Indian rather than for its storytelling
appeal. Here are stories of the origin of rituals, of poor boys and
orphans who obtain medicine power; no Coyote stories are included.
The author's introduction and "Notes on the Pawnees" present rele-
vant background on the Pawnee religion and view of warfare.

84. Lowie, Robert H.
MYTHS AND TRADITIONS OF THE CROW INDIANS. New York, The
Trustees, 1918. 308 p. (Anthropological papers of the American
Museum of Natural History, v. 25, pt. 1)   GN2.A27, v. 25, pt. 1

Bibliography: p. 305–306.

Crow Indian folklore collected in the first decades of the 20th century.
In his introduction Lowie identifies those traits that distinguish Crow
mythology from other Plains Indian mythologies: the popularity of
human heroes, the lack of abstract thought, the absence of tales to
account for the origin of rituals, and a "chaotic assemblage of supernatural and heroic beings." Still, Crow lore is of "emphatically" Plains
Indian cast. The compiler also considers briefly the historical development of Crow mythology, the groups into which the Crows divided
their tales, and how and when they told them. The types of tales
represented are "Old-Man-Coyote Cycle," "Hero Tales," "Tales of
Supernatural Patrons," "Miscellaneous Tales," and "Historical Traditions." They appear here in an unadorned, straightforward style.

85. Parsons, Elsie W. (Clews), *ed.*
KIOWA TALES. New York, American Folklore Society, G. E.
Stechert, agents, 1929. 151 p. (Memoirs of the American Folklore
Society, v. 22)   GR1.A5, v. 22

Folktales and narrative pieces, collected in Oklahoma in 1927, which include some of the many adventures of Sendeh. This trickster-hero, who is said to have gotten things started in the world, is still a "very living figure and freshly borrowed tales might well be fitted to him." Well-known Plains incidents about capturing game account for almost all of the remaining tales in the group. Lacking in storytelling appeal, this lore is, however, brought to life in the *Winter-Telling Stories* (item 93), where the humor and dramatic interest apparent to an Indian audience in the recounting of a familiar incident come through to the modern listener from a more informal, conversational style and a judicious selection and arrangement of the tales. Dr. Parsons' introduction embodies an analysis of the attitudes of informants toward their heritage, a discussion of the traditional narrative style, and comment on the Indian's continued attachment to Sendeh.

86. Wissler, Clark, *and* D. C. Duvall.
   MYTHOLOGY OF THE BLACKFOOT INDIANS. New York, The Trustees, 1908. p. 1–163. (Anthropological papers of the American Museum of Natural History, v. 2, pt. 1)   GN2.A27, v. 2, pt. 1

A collection of tales gathered among the several divisions of the Blackfeet Indians during the years 1903–07, to which is added a background discussion of the Blackfeet mythology.

The introduction treats in some detail the question of the historical evolution of Old Man's character and the surprising variations in detail found in myths associated with sacred rituals.

Narratives "in which the tone of the mythical age predominated, or in which the super-natural was the main interest" were selected for inclusion. Comparative references cite other collections of Blackfeet mythology including that of George B. Grinnell, "by far the most complete collection." The lore is divided into five categories: "Tales of the Old Man," "Star Myths," "Ritualistic Origins," "Cultural and Other Origins," and "Miscellaneous Tales." The last group includes "narratives for children, though all tales of the Old Man are told even to the youngest children, and often recited as lullabies for infants." The narrative style is terse, enlivened by dialogue and song, and with reactions and responses starkly expressed. Dramatic fulfillment, however, is often lacking.

See also item 47, *Indian Legends From the Northern Rockies.*

87. Clay, Charles.
    SWAMPY CREE LEGENDS, BEING TWENTY FOLK TALES FROM THE
    ANNALS OF A PRIMITIVE, MYSTERIOUS, FAST-DISAPPEARING CANADIAN
    RACE, as told to Charles Clay . . . by Kuskapatchees, The Smoky
    One. Toronto, Macmillan, 1938. 95 p. port.   E99.C88C6

Northern Manitoba Swampy Cree legends are presented for children
as they were narrated by an old Indian grandmother. In his preface the
author discusses the narrative style in which the tales had been told,
noting the influence of Biblical prose, the only type of literature to
which these nonliterate people had been exposed. In recording the
stories, he states, "I have in every case chosen the most exciting speci-
men, sometimes even combining especially happy touches."

Wesukechak, a trickster hero who lived long ago and could do all
things, appears as the central character, helping birds and animals as
well as punishing and rewarding them. Because of its fresh handling
of familiar incidents and themes, this collection will appeal to today's
storyteller who enjoys the "fertile resourcefulness of the Indian mind
in explaining the things of life about him."

88. Eastman, Charles A.
    SMOKY DAY'S WIGWAM EVENINGS; INDIAN STORIES RETOLD, by
    Charles A. Eastman (Ohiyesa) and Elaine G. Eastman. Boston,
    Little, Brown, 1910. 148 p. illus.   E98.F6E13

Twenty tales representative of the oral literature of the Sioux are
retold for children in a volume unattractive in format but rewarding
in content. Charles Eastman, a full-blooded Sioux, was introduced to
the folklore of his people in his boyhood by such gifted Indian storytellers as Smoky Day.

In selecting these stories the compilers note that they "have chosen
from a mass of material the shorter and simpler stories and parts of
stories, and have not always insisted upon a literal rendering." They
have purposed "to preserve in the main the true spirit and feeling of
these old tales."

The tales are offered as if presented on consecutive evenings to
children gathered about Smoky Day. The narrative style is simple
and unadorned, the humor and dramatic effect subtly revealed through
the incidents and the characters. Included are animal tales, retold in
the style of a fable; stories of Unktomee, the Spider, wise and cunning,
who could change into a man or animal; hero stories; and stories of
strange beasts, such as Eya the Devourer:

In the old days, longer ago than any one can remember, no one was more feared and dreaded than Eya, the Glutton, the devouring spirit that went to and fro upon the earth, able to draw all living creatures into his hideous, open mouth! His form was monstrous and terrifying. No one seemed to know what he feared, or how he might be overcome. Whole tribes of people were swallowed up by him, and there was no help!

At last came Unktomee, and by his quick wit and genial ways got the better of this enemy of our race.

89. Grinnell, George B.
BLACKFEET INDIAN STORIES. New York, Scribner, 1913. 214 p. col. front. E99.S54G8

Twenty-three stories from the *Blackfoot Lodge Tales; the Story of a Prairie People* (item 81) in a volume designed for younger readers. The original arrangement of the tales has been simplified. Changes in language, while in only a minor way affecting the integrity of the stories, seem unnecessary as weaker words replace stronger and more descriptive ones. Background for the tales is given in brief introductions to individual stories. The final chapter has a description of the country of the Blackfeet and of their traditions and beliefs. This collection deserves to be reissued in a format more attractive to the age group to which the tales will most appeal.

90. Linderman, Frank B.
INDIAN WHY STORIES; SPARKS FROM WAR EAGLE'S LODGE-FIRE, by Frank B. Linderman (Co-skee-see-co-cot) illustrated by Charles M. Russell (Cah-ne-ta-wah-see-na-e-ket) New York, Scribner, 1915. 236 p. E98.F6L7

The stories retold here for children came to the author from the older men of the Blackfeet, Chippewa, and Cree tribes. The Chippewa and Cree had, in fact, adopted him and named him Co-skee-see-co-cot. "Keeping as near as possible to the Indian's style of story-telling," War Eagle, the invented storyteller, relates the lore as if surrounded by his young grandchildren.

Mr. Linderman introduces tales of the creation and of the sometimes humorous, often willful and wily doings of the creator *Old*-man. The author plays with relish upon the many sides of *Old*-man's character. The lively, informal style—as in the stories "*Old*-Man Steals the Sun's Leggings," "The Fire-Leggings," "Why the Deer Has No Gall," and "Why Indians Whip the Buffalo-Berries From the Bushes" —suggests the enthusiastic enjoyment with which these tales must have been told originally. Color plates and black-and-white pencil sketches by a famous cowboy artist depict a spirited and humorous *Old*-man.

Lively animals adorn the halftitle for "Old-Man Remakes the World," one of the Indian Why Stories *by Frank B. Linderman. Charles M. Russell, illustrator, is described as "The Cowboy Artist" on the title page. Item 90.*

The stories in this collection were later reprinted in a school edition, *Indian Lodge-Fire Stories* (New York, Scribner [c1918] E98.F6L68).

A companion volume to *Indian Why Stories, Indian Old-Man Stories; More Sparks From War Eagle's Lodge Fire* (New York, Scribner, 1920. 169 p. E98.F6L69), presented in the same format, does not have the same high level of storytelling interest.

91. ———.

    OLD MAN COYOTE (CROW). Illustrated by Herbert M. Stoops. New York, John Day Co. [c1931] 254 p.   E99.C92L6

On long winter nights the author heard stories from the Crow Indians and set them down "faithfully, just as I got them from Cold-wind, Walks-with-the-wolf, Short-bull, Bird-in-the-ground, Plain-feather, and other old warriors of the tribe, whom I have known for more than forty years."

The tales vary considerably in their appeal. Mr. Linderman describes them as "often without form to me" and indicates that great characters like Sun and Old-man, or Old-man-coyote, have been "confounded." An element of roughness and foul play predominates in the Old-man-coyote stories, while a sense of the dramatic marks such hero tales as "Lodge-Lining and Spring Boy" and tales of the supernatural like "The Two-Faces." The latter tells of a tribe of people with two faces who wager their lives against the lives of their gambling opponents:

Nobody could get behind a Two-face, and nobody could be certain that he was in front of him. This would be bad in gambling! Two eyes can never catch all that four eyes can see.

The length of these stories, told as a succession of adventures, makes them less suited for telling than for reading aloud.

92. Marriott, Alice L.
SAYNDAY'S PEOPLE; THE KIOWA INDIANS AND THE STORIES THEY TOLD. Lincoln, University of Nebraska Press [c1963] 226 p. illus. (A Bison book, BB 174)   E99.K5M358

"Bibliography for Illustrations": p. 223.

Two of the author's books for younger readers, *Winter-Telling Stories* (item 93) and *Indians on Horseback* (New York, Crowell [1948] 136 p. illus. E78.W5M3), are combined to give a well-rounded picture of Plains Indian life as it was. The foreword, containing a brief discussion of the tales' Asiatic roots and the timelessness and universality of the trickster-transformer Saynday and his Euro-American parallels, makes this edition of particular interest to storytellers. The Roland Whitehorse illustrations for *Winter-Telling Stories* have not been reprinted.

93. ———.
WINTER-TELLING STORIES. Illustrations by Roland Whitehorse. New York, W. Sloane Associates [1947] 84 p.   E99.K5M38

Eleven tales collected by a well-known ethnologist concern the colorful Kiowa trickster-transformer Saynday, a tall, thin, "funny-looking man" with a little thin mustache, who could change himself at pleasure into an animal. The author has arranged these tales of bravado and cunning in two groups, "The Saynday-Does-Good Stories" and "The Saynday-Makes-Trouble Stories." Background information appears in brief introductory and concluding sections, "Who Saynday Is and What He Did" and "The End of Saynday." The terse retellings with their clever repartee are full of action and humor. Altogether this excellent collection reveals the wide range of imagination that is possible. Full-page color illustrations by a Kiowa Indian incorporate Plains Indian symbols.

94. Palmer, William R.
WHY THE NORTH STAR STANDS STILL, AND OTHER INDIAN LEGENDS. Illustrated by Ursula Koering. Englewood Cliffs, N.J., Prentice-Hall [1957] 118 p.   E99.P2P33

First published in 1946 with the title: *Pahute Indian legends.*

Stories gathered "over a period of more than a quarter of a century" by the compiler, who knew and worked with the Paiute Indians. The principal characters are the creator Tobats—who made the world, the Indians, and the animals—and his brother Shinob, second in power and greatness. Some are simple "how and why" stories in which the animals figure prominently, and others are historical in character. The inconsistencies in the stories are explained by the compiler: "If the philosophy of one legend conflicts with that of another, the Indian mind is not disturbed. The Indian simply says, 'This is different time.'" The stories have no formal arrangement; they are illustrated with brown-and-white ink drawings of the Indian and animal characters.

95. Penney, Grace J.
TALES OF THE CHEYENNES. Illustrations by Walter R. West. Boston, Houghton Mifflin, 1953. 117 p.   E98.F6P37

A collection of stories "told around Cheyenne campfires when the old men solemnly pass the ceremonial pipe from hand to hand, after a feast." The author's research took her to government reports and ethnological, anthropological, and folklore journals, and she checked her stories with such noted specialists as Alice Marriott "to insure the authenticity of interpretation." However, a bibliography of sources is not included.

Following a short introduction, "How the Cheyenne Stories Are Told," 14 tales are presented in two groups, "Stories of Strange Things" and "Stories of Funny Things." Items in the first group, origin stories of a more serious character, tell of the three heroes, Yellow-Hair, Sweet Medicine, and Standing-on-the-Ground. Into the second group fall the stories of the slapstick adventures of Wihio, a

Saynday was so absorbed in watching field mice have a sun dance inside a buffalo skull that he got stuck in it. The large symbol signifies the trees by which he found his way, moving from species to species. From Winter-Telling Stories *by Alice Marriott; illustrator, Roland Whitehorse. Item 93.*

lazy little man always playing tricks. For her retelling of the origin stories the author has adopted a style that conveys something of the reverent feeling with which the Indians regarded these tales. The Wihio stories have a color and fullness not often found in the originals. These stories, in which corn and the buffalo are characteristic elements, reveal the Indian's preoccupation with getting food and with drought, famine, and the harshness of winter. The black-and-white illustrations by a Cheyenne Indian artist vividly depict incidents and characters.

See also item 64, *The Punishment of the Stingy.*

Central Woodland

The folklore heritage of the Central Woodland that has been passed on to modern boys and girls centers primarily in the figure of Manabozho, the culture hero-trickster, son of the West Wind and great-grandson of thc Moon. In these tales Manabozho appears in the opposite roles of trickster and fool like the Coyote of the West rather than Glooskap of the East. While his name varies slightly in the lore of the different tribes, the basic legends in which he is the central figure are rather consistent. Emphasis on the one culture hero, however, does not take into account the great variety of myth figures that have been identified and that make the Indian mythical world so fantastic and fearful. The hierarchy of supernatural beings in Algonkin mythology ranges from the Great Spirit, Gitche Monedo, through Matche Monedo, the spirit of evil, to the minor deities, the manitos or wizards, and necromancers. Source material in this area indicates that there has been much borrowing from European folklore.

Wihio is the "hero" of the section of Tales of the Cheyennes *called "Stories of Funny Things." Cheyenne artist Walter Richard West has caught him just before he is swallowed by an intended victim. Grace Jackson Penney, author. Item 95.*

96. Barbeau, Charles M.
    HURON AND WYANDOT MYTHOLOGY, WITH AN APPENDIX CONTAINING
    EARLIER PUBLISHED RECORDS. Ottawa, Govt. Print. Bureau, 1915.
    437 p. plates, ports. (Canada. Geological Survey. Memoir 80.
    Anthropological series no. 11)   QE185.A2, no. 80
                                                               E99.H9B2

Myths, tales, and traditions gathered in 1911–12 among halfbreed
Hurons and Wyandots of Quebec, Ontario, and Oklahoma by a re-
nowned Canadian folklorist. Included are "practically all the recorded
Huron and Wyandot mythology, so far as known to the author," with
an appendix of material recorded by missionaries, historians, and
ethnographers in the 17th, 18th, and 19th centuries. Mr. Barbeau's
useful introductory material concerns such topics as the literary style
and antiquity of this body of folklore; themes and episodes and their
diffusion; and a summary of Huron-Wyandot mythology. He notes
that "the scanty and disconnected fragments now preserved from
oblivion in our literature but faintly reveal the significance and grandeur of the native lore taken as a whole." Much that has been recorded
shows the influence of the influx of European tales, riddles, and fables.
    This body of mythology is particularly interesting for its creation
myths. They tell of the woman who fell from heaven and was res-
cued by animals who built an island for her on Big Turtle's back, and
of the work of her twin sons who prepared the world for the coming
of man. Appealing, too, is the association of familiar trickster episodes
in a cycle of Wolf or Fox and Raccoon tales.
    William E. Connelley later published an elaborated and embellished
retelling of these creation myths for young readers in *Indian Myths*
(New York, Rand McNally [c1928] 167 p. Twentieth century classics
and school readings, v. 1, no. 3. E99.H9C68). Mr. Barbeau notes that
Mr. Connelley's work is "somewhat impaired by . . . [his] lack of
scientific accuracy and by his tendency to use the myths which he collected among the western Wyandots as literary material."

97. Radin, Paul, *comp.*
    SOME MYTHS AND TALES OF THE OJIBWA OF SOUTHEASTERN ONTARIO.
    Ottawa, Govt. Print. Bureau, 1914. 83 p. (Canada. Geological Sur-
    vey. Memoir 48; no. 2, Anthropological series)   QE185.A2, no. 48
                                                               E99.C6R13

Forty-five tales gathered in English by Mr. Radin in 1912. Narratives
of Nenebojo, collected from 10 informants, tell of adventures in which
he plays the role of the fool and the trickster. Three versions show how
Nenebojo tricks the geese: by tying their legs together, by rolling them

down the hill in a bag, and by getting them to sing with their eyes
closed. Other stories recount quests and tests of endurance, four of
which are identified as "probably" of European origin.

98. Radin, Paul.
THE TRICKSTER; A STUDY IN AMERICAN INDIAN MYTHOLOGY. With
commentaries by Karl Kerényi and C. G. Jung. London, Routledge
and Paul [1955] 211 p.   E99.W7R142

An ethnologist's scholarly, psychological-literary interpretation of the
trickster cycle of the Winnebago in central Wisconsin and eastern
Nebraska, with comparative discussions of this and other North American Indian trickster cycles. In his literary analysis Mr. Radin describes
the freedom allowed a storyteller in accentuating changes, developing
new styles, and suggesting new interpretations. He considers also the
need for determining which incidents must be included in a particular
cycle of a given tribe and whether they must appear in a certain
sequence. Included in full are the "Winnebago Trickster Cycle" and
the "Winnebago Hare Cycle"; summaries of the Assiniboin and
Tlingit trickster myths follow. A clear study, it is of value to the student of folklore and the teller of trickster tales.

99. ———.
WINNEBAGO HERO CYCLES: A STUDY IN ABORIGINAL LITERATURE.
Baltimore, Waverly Press, 1948. 168 p. (Indiana University pub-
lications in anthropology and linguistics. Memoir 1)
                                   GN4.I5, Memoir 1
                                   E99.W7R145
Bibliographical references included in "Notes" (p. 153–168).

100. ———.
THE CULTURE OF THE WINNEBAGO: AS DESCRIBED BY THEMSELVES.
[Baltimore, Waverly Press, 1949] 119 p. (Indiana University
publications in anthropology and linguistics. Memoir 2)
                                   GN4.I5, Memoir 2

In these two literary analyses of the Winnebago folklore the author
"proceeded on the assumption, unfortunately overtly denied by most
ethnologists, that aboriginal peoples have authentic literatures and
that the literary artists among them are as keenly aware of the literary
qualities of a particular narrative as are our own."
The introduction to the first study describes two categories of Winnebago narrative and the factors bringing about changes in the content
of a myth. Mr. Radin gives four complete cycles collected between

1909 and 1912: "The Trickster Cycle," "The Hare Cycle," "The Red Horn Cycle," and "The Twin Cycle."

In the second work, after background material on the methods of obtaining texts and their translations, appear four tales collected during 1908–18: "The Two Friends Who Became Reincarnated: The Origin of the Four Nights' Wake"; "The Man Who Brought His Wife Back From Spiritland"; "The Journey of the Ghost to Spiritland: As Told in the Medicine Rite"; and "How an Orphan Restored the Chief's Daughter to Life." All of these have an eerie storytelling appeal.

101. Schoolcraft, Henry R.

INDIAN LEGENDS FROM ALGIC RESEARCHES (THE MYTH OF HIA-WATHA, ONEÓTA, THE RED RACE IN AMERICA) AND HISTORICAL AND STATISTICAL INFORMATION RESPECTING THE INDIAN TRIBES OF THE UNITED STATES. Edited by Mentor L. Williams. [East Lansing] Michigan State University Press, 1956. 322 p.   E98.F6S32

Bibliography: p. 320–322.

Mr. Schoolcraft is "the man most responsible for popularizing the oral literature . . . of the aborigine." The poet Henry Wadsworth Longfellow used Mr. Schoolcraft's writings for his *Song of Hiawatha,* wherein the Ojibwa creator-trickster Manabozho is known by an Iroquois name.

This collection brings together in a single volume all the tales gathered and set down by the author in *Algic Researches* (1839), *Oneóta* (1844–45), and *The Myth of Hiawatha* (1856). At the end of every tale is a publication record, noting inclusions in any collection whose compilers acknowledged Mr. Schoolcraft as their source. Two of the collections cited were edited for children: *The Indian Fairy Book, From the Original Legends,* by Florence Choate and Elizabeth Curtis (New York, F. A. Stokes Co. [c1916] 303 p. illus. E98.F6S37), and *The Indian Fairy Book, From the Original Legends,* by Cornelius Mathews (New York, Allen Bros., 1869. 338 p. E98.F6S35). Of these, Mr. Williams notes that "both Matthews [sic] and the Choate-Curtis combination took liberties with the tales that cannot be accepted by anyone who has read the originals"—leaving for a future editor a still unmet challenge. The editor's introduction provides background on Mr. Schoolcraft and his work, while the appendices, with their selections from Mr. Schoolcraft's writings, further describe his theories and concepts of collecting.

The tales reveal a colorful variety of Indian heroes other than the great Manabozho. They describe trials of endurance, the seeking of guardian spirits, and conflicts of braves and poor orphans with powerful manitos and magicians.

Although Mr. Schoolcraft's prose style is simple and flows with ease, his choice of words often reflects the ornate literary mode of his day. As one reviewer noted, "Despite modifications and adaptations, the Schoolcraft collection is a worthy contribution to folk literature. Scientists must use his materials with caution, but it cannot be denied that his tales and legends, however changed, are delightful reading" (*Journal of American Folklore*, v. 70, July/Sept. 1957: 285–286).

102. ————.

THE MYTH OF HIAWATHA, AND OTHER ORAL LEGENDS, MYTHOLOGIC AND ALLEGORIC, OF THE NORTH AMERICAN INDIANS. Philadelphia, Lippincott, 1856. 343 p.   E98.F6S4

In publishing this collection Mr. Schoolcraft attempted to gain a kind of popular recognition that he had not yet received. In 1855 Longfellow published *Hiawatha* and, as Mentor Williams noted (item 101), "the public reception was so overwhelming that Schoolcraft decided the profit from such popularity should not all go into the Cambridge poet's pocket. He prepared a new and slightly modified collection of the tales, adding many from *Oneóta* and omitting some from *Algic Researches*, identified the stories boldly with Hiawatha, and published the work under the title, *The Myth of Hiawatha*, in 1856. Even with the fillip afforded by Longfellow's book, the public failed to respond and a second edition was not needed."

103. Skinner, Alanson B., *and* John V. Satterlee.

FOLKLORE OF THE MENOMINI INDIANS. New York, The Trustees, 1915. p. 217–546. (Anthropological papers of the American Museum of Natural History, v. 13, pt. 3)   GN2.A27, v. 13, pt. 3
                                                          E99.M44S6

Bibliography: p. 544–546.

"Typical tales" from the folklore and mythology of the Menominee, a tribe of the Great Lakes region, collected during the summers of 1910–14. Introductory background material includes such lists as "Popular Types of Action," found in the folklore of the Menominee and other central Algonkin tribes, and "Stereotyped Properties and Tools" ("mechanical objects or tools associated with the actors in the tales just as in European lore the witch always appears with her broomstick or her black cat"). Briefly discussed are the "Characteristic Traits of Menomini Folklore," "Customs Concerning Narration," and "Informants and Methods."

Represented in these papers are tales about Mä'näbus as the culture hero and as fool and trickster; accounts of imaginary heroes; true stories, being "tales of the warpath, the chase, in love, supernatural adventures, dreams, conjuring, and exploits of animals and persons"; and stories of "undoubted European origin." A final section summarizes some of the tales and compares specific incidents identified in other collections of Indian lore. In general, the tales are presented in an informal conversational style. Of particular interest are the occasional uncommon incidents, as in the "Deluge" story when "the beings above challenged the beings below to a mighty game of lacrosse."

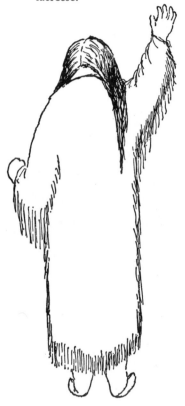

Two illustrations from The World of Manabozho *by Thomas B. Leekley. Illustrator Yeffe Kimball was influenced by Eastern Woodland Indian birchbark drawings. Item 105. Left, Nakomis— Manabozho's grandmother—bids him farewell as he embarks to find his father, Wabun, the West Wind. Manabozho is determined to find out the story of his mother and her whereabouts and avenge her death if necessary. Opposite, Manabozho rescues animals from "The Flood," a universal deluge which gushed out of the wigwam where Manabozho slew his nephew's murderer. He creates a new world to solve this problem.*

Children's Editions

104. Davis, Susan B.
WISCONSIN LORE FOR BOYS AND GIRLS. [Eau Claire, Wis.] E. M. Hale, 1931. 283 p. illus. F581.D28

This history of the State of Wisconsin contains a small selection of Algonkin Indian tales, principally those of the Chippewa. The author acknowledges such sources as United States Ethnological Reports and works by Henry R. Schoolcraft and other Indian folklore specialists. She has treated faithfully the tales selected from Schoolcraft collections. A few stories such as "The Rabbit and Saw-Whit Owl" and "Shingebiss" could be enjoyed by boys and girls in the story hour today.

105. Leekley, Thomas B.

THE WORLD OF MANABOZHO; TALES OF THE CHIPPEWA INDIANS.
With illustrations by Yeffe Kimball. New York, Vanguard Press
[1965] 128 p.   E99.C6L37

The Chippewa and Ottawa are the "living owners" of these tales that
"had their origins around the lodge fires of the Algonquian family of
Indian tribes." The author notes that "related tales appear in the
mythologies of such distant relatives as the Blackfoot of Montana and
the Cree of Hudson Bay." From the great collection of "anecdotes,
episodes, jokes, and fables" found in Indian folklore, the author has
had to "rearrange and edit" his material to arrive at "finished stories."
In a final section he describes the liberties he took in editing and indicates where he has altered the traditional arrangement of the Manabozho tales in order to show a development of character. He presents
the last four Manabozho stories as a hero cycle telling of Manabozho's
search for his brother and of his desire to avenge his mother's death.
Other humorous stories depict the adventures of Wiskedjak, the
Canadian jay. The simple, rhythmic prose, evoking a mood and atmosphere of the lake country, is well suited to storytelling, as in "The
Theft of Fire":

> One day in early winter, soon after Manabozho had grown to manhood, he
> stood before his grandmother's wigwam shivering in the bitter wind. The lake
> was frozen. The sun, a pale yellow disk, had lost its heat. He shivered again,
> knowing that for many months his lodge would be cold, his food frozen, his drink-
> ing water underneath four feet of solid ice.
> "Nakomis, old grandmother," he said sadly, "I have heard that once, long ago,
> people had heat within their wigwams all the year. Is it true?"

The artist's black-and-white line drawings were inspired by the
Eastern Woodland Indians' incised and colored birchbark drawings.

106. Reid, Dorothy M.

TALES OF NANABOZHO. Illustrated by Donald Grant. New York,
Walck, 1963. 128 p.   E99.C6R32

Bibliography: p. [127]–128.

Twenty-one tales of the Ojibwa "creator-magician," son of the West
Wind and great-grandson of the Moon. The author, a Canadian children's librarian, states that in her "retellings" she has "used incidents
from the mythology both of the Ojibwa and of other tribes in the
Algonkian language group to which the Ojibwa belong."
The stories range from the time of Nanabozho's birth and his later
winning of Minnehaha, Laughing Water, as his bride, to the coming
of the white man when the Great Spirit cast a spell over Nanabozho
and he fell eternally asleep. Into these short tales, which are identified

Some Indians say that geese have flown in a V ever since Nanabozho tried to trap an entire flock of resting geese by tying their feet together under the water. The would-be trapper was forced to go along for a ride when the geese discovered their plight and flew off, still fastened by the bark rope. From Tales of Nanabozho *written by Dorothy M. Reid and illustrated by Donald Grant. Item 106.*

with familiar geographical landmarks of the Great Lakes area, Mrs. Reid has woven Indian "how and why" beliefs. Her prose style is simple and clear, evoking a sense of sympathy for the human characters, as illustrated in "How Nanabozho Brought Fire to His People":

In the early days of the world the people had no fire to warm them and to cook their food. Because they saw its destructive power when lightning set the forest ablaze, they were afraid of it.

Once the Coyote went to the underworld and brought back a brand of fire for the tribes. But the people forbade its use and appointed an old warrior-magician to watch over it. Some fearless braves tried to steal it for themselves, but it was always well guarded by the magician and his two fierce daughters.

As Nanabozho himself was young and strong, the lack of fire for heat did not trouble him particularly. His grandmother, however, was growing old and felt the cold severely. In the winter she spent much of the time huddled in her fur robe complaining bitterly.

Nanabozho entered the wigwam one day and, finding her thus, sought to cheer her.

The strong, stylized ink drawings portray Nanabozho as a stalwart young brave.

107. Walker, Bertrand N. O.
TALES OF THE BARK LODGES, by Hen-Toh, Wyandot. Oklahoma City, Harlow Pub. Co. [c1919] 107 p.   E98.F6W25

The "Ol' Fox an' Ol' Coon" cycle and other Wyandot folktales told in the "broken dialect peculiar alone to the 'old time Indian.'"

Mr. Barbeau's collection, *Huron and Wyandot Mythology* (item 96), contains the same Fox-Raccoon cycle also presented in an informal conversational style, but without the distraction of the broken dialect. Familiar episodes in the cycle include a variant of the widely known "Why the Bear Has a Stumpy Tail," elements common to the Uncle Remus stories, and incidents relating to the dancing geese. Potentially good storytelling material, these tales await a less affected manner of treatment.

See also item 96, *Huron and Wyandot Mythology;* item 101, *Indian Legends From Algic Researches.*

Northeast Woodland

The popularity of tales of a culture hero, a pattern that emerges in many culture areas represented in this bibliography, is seen also in collections of eastern Algonkin folklore for children. For each children's edition listed, the name of the creator-culture-hero, Glooskap, appears in the title. He is characterized by Charles Leland (item 109) as benevolent and never devoid of dignity, one who never, "like the Manobozho-Hiawatha of the Chippewas, becomes silly, cruel, or fantastic." In physical stature he can be like a giant, rising to the clouds, his head touching the stars. Among the tales of his exploits is a unique group relating to his departure to another world and to the adventurers who seek him out in order to have their one wish granted.

Charles Leland and Silas Rand, pioneer collectors of Northeast Woodland lore, produced the earliest and two most frequently cited sources. However, their works stand in contrast to later, more objective field-collected texts, which criticize those early collections for their lack of an "originality that every reader feels the true examples of native oral literature should possess." In these latter collections is recorded fresh, lively material that will be of interest to students and compilers of folklore. A European influence, particularly of the French, is very strong in these tales. Some are wholly European; others, while European in theme, with Old World characters and plots, have Indian heroes and characters who react in a manner that is true to Indian custom.

108. Beck, Horace P.

GLUSKAP THE LIAR, & OTHER INDIAN TALES. With illustrations by Arthur K. D. Healy. Freeport, Me., B. Wheelwright [c1966] 282 p.   E99.P5B4

Bibliography: p. 178–182.

A brief study, from a folklorist's point of view, of the history and culture of the Penobscot Indians of Maine, with folklore chosen to illustrate various aspects of their life. The author has selected lively myths, tales, and narratives from field-collected texts and records set down by early explorers. He states that whenever material has numerous analogues in printed sources, he has set down only the gist of a tale; when the material is not widely known, he has preserved the original phraseology but has given it a more grammatically correct form. In a section of notes, motifs and sources of individual tales are discussed in some detail. This general introduction to the lore of the Northeast Woodland tribes indicates the interest that the material holds for students and future compilers of folklore.

109. Leland, Charles G.

THE ALGONQUIN LEGENDS OF NEW ENGLAND; OR, MYTHS AND FOLK LORE OF THE MICMAC, PASSAMAQUODDY, AND PENOBSCOT TRIBES. London, S. Low, Marston, Searle & Rivington, 1884. 379 p. plates.   E98.F6L5 1884a

This writer of humorous verse and student of gypsy folklore began collecting the tales and traditions of the Passamaquoddy at Campobello, New Brunswick, in 1882. The legends in this collection, which he describes as "fragmentary and incomplete," were "taken down from the trembling memories of old squaws who never understood their inner meaning, or from ordinary *senaps* who had not thought of them since boyhood." He also made use of a manuscript of 84 Micmac tales gathered by the Reverend Silas T. Rand.

To support his theory of the Norse origin of northeastern Algonkin folklore, Mr. Leland, in his introduction, makes detailed comparisons to the Eddas and Eskimo myths and tales. In notes following individual stories he considers their antiquity and probable origins.

"What is tickling my legs?" Glooscap in disguise as the Green Giant laughs down at Badger and stuffs Badger's Little Brother into his basket. Glooscap is about to teach Badger a lesson for tricking his tribe out of their food. From Glooscap and His Magic *by Kay Hill, illustrated by Robert Frankenberg. Item 112.*

Included are stories of Glooskap, the central figure of northeastern Algonkin mythology—always benevolent, never cruel, silly, or devoid of dignity. Other accounts tell of the adventures of Lox, the Mischief-maker; Master Rabbit or Mahtigwees; the Chenoo, a cannibal with an icy heart; At-o-sis, a serpent; and Partridge, or Pulowech. These tales are potentially good storytelling material, a few of them as complete tales—for example, "How Glooskap Conquered the Great Bull-Frog" —and others for episodes and details.

Mr. Speck (item 111), in describing Charles Leland's methods of collecting, notes that the myths "are not presented objectively enough nor recorded critically enough to be of much value for comparison." Though Mr. Leland's style of telling is embellished and highly personal, his enthusiasm for all the subtleties of a good story is charming.

Some of these tales are included in *Kulóskap the Master and Other Algonkin Poems* (New York, Funk & Wagnalls Co., 1902. 370 p. illus. E98.F6L56). These metrical versions were prepared by Charles Leland and then revised and corrected by Professor John D. Prince, who compared them with original texts he had gathered in his linguistic research among the Canadian Abnaki.

110. Rand, Silas T.
    Legends of the Micmacs. [Edited by Helen L. Webster] New York, Longmans, Green, 1894. 452 p. port. (Wellesley philological publications)   E99.M6R1

Folklore recorded during the 40 years, beginning in 1846, that Dr. Rand spent among the Micmac Indians of Nova Scotia as a missionary and a linguist. Shortly after his death his Indian manuscripts were acquired by Wellesley College where Helen L. Webster of the Department of Comparative Philology prepared them for publication, preserving, "as nearly as possible, the wording of the original." She has added extensive introductory material describing Dr. Rand's methods of collecting and his observations of these primitive people and their culture.

These stories were related to Dr. Rand in Micmac and then translated and written down by him in English. The narration in the original language has not been preserved. The period covered ranges from "Ancient Times" to events that took place since the coming of the white man and the Indian's conversion to Christianity, as indicated by the many European tales remodeled into the "Indian style of the marvelous." Included are stories of Glooscap; Kītpooseāgūnow, a hero who resembles Glooscap; Kekwajoo (Badger); Ābīstānaooch (Marten); Ableegumooch (Rabbit); and many stories of war. Accounts of a single myth figure are not grouped together. The style of telling is simple and unadorned, the narrative interspersed with Dr.

Rand's occasional remarks on native manners and customs. This collection parallels Mr. Leland's (item 109), though there is variance in
the sequence and choice of episodes and the fullness of detail with
which an event is related.

111. Speck, Frank G.
    PENOBSCOT TRANSFORMER TALES. International journal of Ameri-
    can linguistics, v. 1, Aug. 1918: 187–244.   PM101.I5, v. 1

Mythological texts collected early in this century and prepared by an
ethnologist working with an Indian raconteur are given in the original
language with interlinear and free translations. The short introduction
will interest students of folklore, for the author comments on the
range in the sequence and choice of episodes in the Glooskap cycle
and on this hero's mixed role of "shaman, trickster, and somewhat
altruistic culture hero" in the Penobscot versions. Of northeastern
Algonkin folklore published in earlier collections, he notes, "without
exception, it has been interpreted and rendered in an altered form."
    This collection includes "Tales of Gluskạ'be 'The Deceiver,'"
"Secondary Myths Concerning Gluskạ'be," and "Secondary Hero-
Transformer Tales." The style of telling is simple, clear, and enlivened
by conversation. Neither the versions of "Gluskạ'be Bags All the Game-
Animals" nor of "Gluskạ'be Traps All the Fish" appear in editions
for children appropriate to this culture area. "Gluskạ'be Tempers the
Wind" is told with notable freshness of detail.

Children's Editions

112. Hill, Kay.
    GLOOSCAP AND HIS MAGIC; LEGENDS OF THE WABANAKI INDIANS.
    Illustrated by Robert Frankenberg. New York, Dodd, Mead
    [1963] 189 p.   E99.A13H5

Abnaki "atookwakuns"—marvelous stories of giants, wizards, and
magical animals—originally prepared for a series of television story
hours. The compiler, a script writer for radio and television, has freely
adapted and interpreted the tales collected by Mr. Leland and Mr.
Rand. She explains that it was necessary "to tighten plots, develop
characterization, and invent incidents to explain motivation" in order
to present the stories in a form to which "children today are accus-
tomed." All the tales, including the trickster tales of Rabbit and Badger
and those of European origin, are identified with Glooscap, who
appears disguised in many forms, rewarding and punishing his people.
Because of the exaggerated action and lack of subtlety in this collec-

tion, it will appeal to younger children. The pencil sketches depict the various animals, giants, and Indians in the stories.

Related in a similar style is the author's *Badger, the Mischief Maker* (New York, Dodd, Mead [1965] 95 p. illus. E99.A13H47), a single story incorporating the many exploits of this wily trickster.

113. Macmillan, Cyrus.
GLOOSKAP'S COUNTRY, AND OTHER INDIAN TALES. Illustrated by John A. Hall. Toronto, New York, Oxford University Press, 1956. 273 p.   E98.F6M18

A reprinting in a single volume of two earlier collections of folklore gathered from various parts of Canada: *Canadian Fairy Tales* (New York, Dodd, Mead [1922] 203 p. illus. GR113.M25) and *Canadian Wonder Tales* (London, John Lane; New York, John Lane Co., 1918. 199 p. illus. GR113.M3).

In the original introductions, which have not been reprinted, Professor Macmillan explains that these tales were gathered directly from the people—"nameless Indians and 'habitants' "—for a collection of folktales and folksongs intended for "more academic and scientific purposes." In adapting them for children "the skeleton of each story has been left unchanged." Included is a tale of Raven from the North Pacific Coast and tales from the Canadian plains where the Blackfeet roamed. Most of the stories can be identified with the lore of the eastern Algonkin but also incorporate incidents from other areas. An attempt has been made to group the tales by type. Many of Glooskap's adventures are presented in one long narrative, a few in individual stories. Mr. Macmillan's trickster tales of Rabbit (also known as Mahtigwees or Master Rabbit), like the Fox and Raccoon tales of the Huron and Wyandot, contain a version of "Why the Bear Has a Stumpy Tail" and elements common to the Brer Rabbit stories.

The author's warm, simple style made this book worthy of selection for the Book of the Year Award by Canadian Children's Librarians in 1956. However, it lacks folkloristic notes giving background of the source material. Spirited red-and-black ink drawings have replaced the soft watercolor plates of the earlier collections.

114. Partridge, Emelyn N.
GLOOSCAP THE GREAT CHIEF, AND OTHER STORIES; LEGENDS OF THE MICMACS. New York, Sturgis & Walton Co., 1913. 293 p. port., plates.   E99.M6P2

Faithful renderings of Dr. Rand's tales by a storyteller who as a child heard the stories of Glooscap directly from Dr. Rand, a family visitor. As her main source she cites his *Legends of the Micmacs* (item 110) and also acknowledges some use of Charles Leland's *The Algonquin*

Frontispiece to Glooscap and His Magic *by illustrator Robert Frankenberg; author, Kay Hill. Item 112.*

Legends of New England (item 109) and *Kulóskap the Master* by Charles Leland and John Prince (item 109). Her introduction offers information on the history of the Micmacs and the origin of their legends as well as brief descriptions of the types of stories recorded by Dr. Rand. Thirty-nine of his 87 stories are given, grouped as "Wonder Tales of the Forest"; "Animal Stories (The Adventure of Ableegumooch, The Rabbit, and The Adventures of the Badger)"; "Fairy Tales"; and "Legends of Glooscap the Great Chief." The omission of Dr. Rand's personal comments and ethnological remarks interspersed in his narrative, and the occasional retelling of one incident from a long narrative make this material better for storytelling.

Iroquois

This is an area in which the richness of recorded folklore is not reflected in editions for children. The four collections representing original source material contain stories obtained from Indian informants and include a significant number of tales of heroic encounters with supernatural powers, witches, giants, and personified forces of nature. They are conceived with a boldness of plot and imagination that would appeal to older boys and girls. In contrast with other parts of North America, the number of animal tales recorded in this area is small.

115. Converse, Harriet (Maxwell).
MYTHS AND LEGENDS OF THE NEW YORK IROQUOIS. Edited and anotated [sic] by Arthur C. Parker. Port Washington, N.Y., I. J. Friedman, 1962. 195 p. illus., ports. (Empire State historical publication, 7)   E99.I7C79

"Originally published in 1908 as New York State Museum Bulletin No. 125."

Folklore collected by Mrs. Converse in the last half of the 19th century during the 22 years of her adopted life among the Seneca Indians. The editor, an anthropologist descended from a Seneca Indian chief, has provided a brief introduction to Iroquois folklore, a biographical sketch of Mrs. Converse, bibliographical footnotes, and notes to explain obscure passages in the tales. In describing the compiler's methods, he states that she attempted "to produce the same emotions in the mind of civilized man which is produced in the primitive mind, which entertains the myth without destroying the native style or warping the facts of the narrative." Part 1 reproduces a manuscript of 22 legends found among Mrs. Converse's papers, and additional material prepared from her notes by the editor. The tales in part 2 were revised from rough drafts found among her manuscripts, and part 3 is a collection of miscellaneous papers describing Indian traditions. Stories are varied in character: "Gus-Tah-Ote, Spirit of the Rock" is a sensitive tale of a spirit imprisoned in a rock since the beginning of the earth; "Ga-Do-Jih and Sa-Go-Da-Oh, the Golden Eagle and the Hunter Vulture, Origin of the Bird Dance" tells why these ravenous birds are not denied "the pure air of the sky nor the clear waters of the earth"; while "Ko-Nea-Raw-Neh, the Flying Heads" is a chilling account of a woman pursued by a supernatural power that meets its doom, never to return.

116. Curtin, Jeremiah, *and* John N. B. Hewitt, *comps.*
SENECA FICTION, LEGENDS, AND MYTHS. Edited by J. N. B. Hewitt. *In* U.S. *Bureau of American Ethnology.* Annual report. 32d; 1910/11. Washington, 1918. p. 37–819.   E51.U55 32d
                                                                      E99.S3C92

Folklore collected by Jeremiah Curtin among the Senecas of New York in 1883, 1886, and 1887, to which is added a series of tales recorded by Mr. Hewitt in 1896. In his lengthy folkloristic introduction characterizing the contents of the collection, the editor quotes from writings of Mr. Curtin that analyze and interpret the legends and myths he gathered. Mr. Hewitt then discusses his interpretation of the process of mythmaking as a substitution of human heroes for the personified forces or processes of nature. The collection consists largely of narratives classified as tales of fiction, "naïve productions of the story-teller's art" containing "many things that characterize myths." They relate the encounters of human heroes, who possess magic powers or *orenda,* with phenomena of nature in human guise or in that of birds or beasts (for example, the Stone Coats or Stone Giants, the Thunder People, the Whirlwind People, the Wind People).

Franz Boas considers this work "the most important source–book for Iroquois folklore," revealing that the "Iroquois have developed a strong individuality in the formation of the plots and in the literary treatment of their mythology" (*Journal of American Folklore,* v. 32, July/Sept. 1919, p. 445–446).

117. Curtin, Jeremiah, *comp.*
    SENECA INDIAN MYTHS. New York, Dutton [c1923] 516 p.
    E98.F6C9

"The Indian myths here presented, in their original form as dictated to Mr. Curtin by aged Indians of the Seneca people, were collected by him while acting as an agent of the Bureau of Ethnology of the Smithsonian Institute [sic]." Many of these tales first appeared in an annual report of the U.S. Bureau of American Ethnology (item 116). Typical of the collection as a whole is the story of "The Grandmother and Grandson," simply told, imaginatively conceived, with sustained dramatic interest; the action derives from situations found in many of the tales—traveling in a forbidden direction, encounters with powerful beings, and tests of endurance. In contrast is the charming riddle, "A Bird in Search of a Mate." This posthumous volume of Seneca Indian myths makes more accessible an important and interesting body of folklore.

118. Parker, Arthur C.
    SENECA MYTHS AND FOLK TALES. Buffalo, N.Y., Buffalo Historical Society, 1923. 465 p. illus. (Buffalo Historical Society. Publications, v. 27)   F129.B8B88, v. 27

Bibliography: p. 459.

A representative collection of Seneca folklore recorded in 1903 and 1904 from Edward Cornplanter and other Indian informants, with introductory material useful for the storyteller and student of folklore. Following a general discussion of methods of recording and transcribing folklore are a summary of the Iroquoian cosmology, descriptions of the chief mythological beings, and lists of the characteristic types of action and magical objects that occur in the tales. The stories are grouped under the following headings: "When the World Was New," "Boys Who Defied Magic and Overcame It," "Tales of Love and Marriage," "Horror Tales of Cannibals and Sorcerers," "Tales of Talking Animals," "Tales of Giants," "Pygmies and Monster Bears," and "Traditions."

In a note to the general reader, Mr. Parker cautions that "if readings from this book are to be made for children, a wise selection must be made." It is, however, a readable collection offering interesting variant material.

The author, whose boyhood was spent among the Seneca Indians, edited two collections for children: *Skunny Wundy and Other Indian Tales* (New York, George H. Doran Co. [c1926] 262 p. E98.F6P15) and *Rumbling Wings and Other Indian Tales* (Garden City, N.Y., Doubleday, Doran, 1928. 279 p. E98.F6P14). Other than the myths and legends, which did not change, he notes that "there was also fiction that a story-teller weaves as he goes." The lore in these two collections is presented "not in the Indian tongue or even in the exact way that Indians [told] them, but in the way that boys and girls of to-day will understand." In spirit, these tales do not have the same appeal as those gathered directly from the Indian raconteurs.

Children's Editions

See item 118, *Seneca Myths and Folk Tales.*

Southeast

The trickster tales of Rabbit and similar animal tales hold a prominent place in the folklore of the Indians of the Southeast. These stories are of the same type made popular by Joel Chandler Harris in his Uncle Remus tales. Ethnologists have noted a strong resemblance to stories found in African and European folklore and to the medieval animal epics and fables. A claim is also made for an American Indian origin. Editions of southeastern folklore retold for children, while few in number, present a representative selection of sacred tales and humorous "how and why" stories. The collection made by James Mooney in the 19th century has been a basic source for compilers and can still be referred to for fresh material. This extensive collection is complemented by smaller, more recent gatherings of folklore that include details recorded for the first time—as a song interpolated in the telling of a story or a unique retelling by a gifted storyteller.

119. Davis, John B.
Some Cherokee stories. Annals of archaeology and anthropology, v. 3, June 1910: 26–29. GN1.A6, v. 3

The author, himself of Cherokee descent and familiar with the Cherokee language, presents 22 short tales in a satisfying storytelling style. Mr. Davis says of these stories, "They are genuine. I have not doctored them in any way. . . . The language is very figurative, and a literal translation would not be intelligible to anyone except a Cherokee, or some one very familiar with them." The trickster element predominates, with the tricked animal often reciprocating the tricks of the trickster. Though most of these tales of the western Cherokee are represented in the collection made among the eastern Cherokee by James Mooney (item 122), this author's personal narrative style, combination of episodes, and selection of details enhance his versions.

120. Jarrett, Robert F.
Occoneechee, the maid of the mystic lake. New York, Shakespeare Press, 1916. 284 p. E99.C5J37

This collection is of interest for the small selection of tales—sacred myths, animal stories, local legends, and historical traditions—taken from James Mooney's extensive collection (item 122). "Occoneechee," an original poem by the author, a native of North Carolina, is a romantic account of the Cherokee's tragic removal to the Indian Territory.

121. Kilpatrick, Jack F., *and* Anna G. Kilpatrick, *eds. and trs.*
Friends of Thunder, folktales of the Oklahoma Cherokees. Dallas, Southern Methodist University Press [1964] 197 p. E99.C5K48

In 1961, when Mr. Kilpatrick, himself of Cherokee descent, collected this material from the tribe in Oklahoma, there was a feeling among the Indians that "the art of storytelling among the Cherokees had fallen upon evil, perhaps final days." In his short introductions to the groups of tales, he compares his versions—many of them fragmentary, though some details are recorded here for the first time—with the earlier, more extensive collection of James Mooney (item 122), John Swanton (item 123), and others. In the section of "Tseg'sgin' Stories" are a number of tales identified as European in origin.

122. Mooney, James.
MYTHS OF THE CHEROKEE. *In* U.S. *Bureau of American Ethnology.*
Annual report. 19th; 1897/98. Washington, 1900. pt. 1, p. 3–568,
569*–576*.   E51.U55 19th

An extensive collection of myths and traditions gathered during the
years 1887 to 1890 from the Cherokee living on the Qualla Reservation
in North Carolina and in various detached settlements. The tales were
related by John Ax and other old men of the tribe. They had heard
them as boys while tending the fires of the "myth-keepers and priests"
who met together at night to recite the traditions. Other stories, told
to while away the long evenings, are humorous explanations of certain
animal peculiarities. Background information following a long historical sketch includes a discussion of the types of tales and of the
relationship between the Indian myths and the stories of southern
Negroes. Both groups accord a prominent place in their lore to the
rabbit as a trickster and mischiefmaker. The material is grouped as
"Cosmogonic Myths," "Quadruped Myths," "Bird Myths," "Snake,
Fish, and Insect Myths," "Wonder Stories," "Historical Traditions,"
and "Miscellaneous Myths and Legends." Summaries of the folk beliefs associated with individual animals precede some groups of tales.
In a final section are additional background notes and references to
variants in other collections.

These tales are presented in a quiet, descriptive style, with a satisfying fullness of detail. However, the strength of the plots varies greatly.
This collection, still the one most frequently cited by compilers of
Cherokee folklore, remains a rewarding source of original stories,
such as this version of "The Daughter of the Sun," which is not included in available collections for children:

> Now, the Sun hated the people on the earth, because they could never look
> straight at her without screwing up their faces. She said to her brother, the Moon,
> "My grandchildren are ugly; they grin all over their faces when they look at me."
> But the Moon said, "I like my younger brothers; I think they are very handsome"—
> because they always smiled pleasantly when they saw him in the sky at night, for
> his rays were milder.

123. Swanton, John R.
MYTHS AND TALES OF THE SOUTHEASTERN INDIANS. Washington,
U.S. Govt. Print. Off., 1929. 275 p. (Smithsonian Institution.
Bureau of American Ethnology. Bulletin 88)   E51.U6, no. 88
                                                          E98.F6S92

The greater part of this material was collected by the author between
1908 and 1914 from Creek, Hitchiti, Alabama, Koasati, and Natchez
Indians living in Oklahoma, Texas, and Louisiana. Tales organized
in five tribal collections are followed by a list of the 79 stories—for

example, "Crane and Humming Bird Race," "Terrapin Races," "Rabbit Fools Alligator," "Rabbit Rides Wolf," "The Tar Baby," "Rabbit
Ties an Animal to a Horse," "Rabbit Gets Some One to Hold Up the
Tree"—to which is added the number of different tellings recorded
for each tribe. Of interest to the compiler of folklore and the storyteller is the number of incidents relating to the southeastern trickster,
Rabbit, including borrowings and those of modern origin. The reader
is referred to Stith Thompson's *European Tales Among the North
American Indians* (item 8) for background on the European origin
of the "Rabbit" stories.

Children's Editions

124. Bailey, Carolyn S.
    STORIES FROM AN INDIAN CAVE; THE CHEROKEE CAVE BUILDERS.
    Illustrated by Joseph E. Dash. Chicago, A. Whitman [c1924]
    217 p. illus. (part col.)   E98.F6B2

An early collection of Cherokee lore retold for younger boys and girls
by a well-established writer of children's books. She notes that these
are the tales preserved in scholarly collections made by the "Government at Washington" as gathered from John Ax and other Indians
who heard them when they were young boys tending the fires in
storytellers' lodges (see item 122). Mrs. Bailey's informal storytelling
style is best suited to the humorous trickster tales of Rabbit. While
there is occasional sentimentalizing, in general the versions retain the
spirit of the originals.

125. Bell, Corydon.
    JOHN RATTLING-GOURD OF BIG COVE; A COLLECTION OF CHEROKEE
    INDIAN LEGENDS. New York, Macmillan, 1955. 103 p.   E99.C5B38

The folklore of the author's Cherokee neighbors is still being related
to the children by the old people on the Qualla Indian Reservation at
Cherokee, North Carolina. Many of these legends, recorded by a school
librarian on the reservation, differ only in detail from the stories gathered earlier by James Mooney (item 122). The 24 myths and legends
are presented as if being told by John Rattling-Gourd to his young
friends on the reservation, and the author has "been careful to accu-
rately retain the details and spirit, as well as much of the wording of
the originals." The tales are principally "how and why" stories in
which the animals, birds, and plants come to be as we know them.
They relate to children's everyday interests and recall the days when

the animals were believed to be like men—but of a lesser degree—belonging to tribes, holding council, and playing games. Here are stories of the clever Rabbit and the tricks he plays on Possum, Terrapin, and others; in another vein is the tale of the terrible witch, Spearfinger. Detailed black-and-white line drawings imaginatively capture the mood and flavor of the action.

125a. Mooney, James.
CHEROKEE ANIMAL TALES. Edited with introduction by George F. Scheer. Illustrated by Robert Frankenberg. New York, Holiday House [c1968] 79 p.   E99.C5M77

Thirteen short tales selected by an American history specialist from the James Mooney collection (item 122). In this edition the stories have not undergone the editorial embellishment characteristic of other collections prepared for children, such as those of Bailey (item 124) and Bell (item 125), which are based on the same source. Mr. Scheer remarks: "Essentially, these simple but robust little tales appear here just as they were told originally to James Mooney by the Cherokee and set down by his pen." In his background information Mr. Scheer discusses the role of the animals in Cherokee folklore, noting that the most prominent figure is Rabbit, the trickster and deceiver, who is often beaten at his own games by those whom he intended to victimize. Soft, realistic pencil sketches capture the humor inherent in these tales.

The witch, U-tlun-ta or Spearfinger, prowled the woods searching for food—fresh human livers, especially the tender livers of children! The hunter, hiding to escape her notice, observed the witch in her true form as she passed by chanting lowly: "Uwe-la na-tsi-ku, liver, I eat it. Uwe-la na-tsi-ku." Spearfinger's skin was hard as rock and repelled all arrows and spears. Her flinty forefinger always pointed outward from her fist. Transformed into another guise, she would approach her victim and use her lethal forefinger to remove his liver painlessly, leaving no wound. The unsuspecting victim would later sicken and die, and no one could name the cause. When the Cherokee finally discovered that she carried her heart inside her closed fist, they shot an arrow through it. From John Rattling-Gourd of Big Cove, written and illustrated by Corydon Bell. Item 125.

Southwest

The extensive, rich oral literature of the Southwest includes a general origin myth, chantways (a type of ceremonial lore), and what has been called the "novelistic type tale distinctive in Indian folklore." The general origin myth recounts events of the emergence of the race from the underworld and the exploits of the War Gods engaged in ridding the world of monsters. Branching off from this general origin myth are the myths associated with rituals; in these, many of the same episodes recur. Each ritual or chantway has its own myth telling how the ceremony was obtained from supernatural beings through the trials of a hero. Drawing upon this sacred lore are subsidiary narratives or folktales intended to entertain or teach a moral. They include fictionalized versions of native life; it has been suggested that these have been influenced by the European type of "fairy tale." Exploits of Coyote are told both as part of the general origin myth and as animal trickster tales.

The source material listed incorporates, in addition to the tales themselves, discussions of the techniques and devices of the Indian story-teller and examples of the vivid or subtle expression of the Indian narrative style. Editions for children, many of which are retellings of lore related to the compilers by native storytellers, present the tales contained in the general origin myth in varied arrangements and also in a secular style.

126. Benedict, Ruth F.
ZUNI MYTHOLOGY. New York, Columbia University Press, 1935.
2 v. 344, 347 p. (Columbia University contributions to anthropology, v. 21)   E51.C7, v. 21
                                                                 E99.Z9B4

Contents.—v. 1. Introduction.—The emergence and other Kachina tales.—Ahaiyute adventures.—Tales of courtship.—v. 2. Tales of despised and unacknowledged children.—Tales of husbands and wives.—Tales of conflicts with witches.—Tales of war and famine.—Animal tales.—Miscellaneous tales.

Tales collected by Dr. Benedict at Zuñi in 1922 and 1923 form a useful source book of Zuñi mythology and concordance of Pueblo Indian folktales. In the final section of each volume this well-known anthropologist supplies "abstracts of all Zuñi versions of all tales, and comparative discussion of these versions." In the introduction she discusses two problems in detail: the themes that Zuñi folklore elaborate and their relation to the culture; and the literary problems of the Zuñi narrator—his role, the fixed limits within which he works, and his stylistic aims. By means of examples, she illustrates how compensatory daydreaming and mythological exaggeration function in the process of Zuñi mythmaking. Enjoyably rendered in an unadorned prose style, these stories exhibit what the editor describes as the "general mildness" of Zuñi tales. Plots are constructed by the combination and recombination of traditional incidents—given in the "Index of Incidents"—and developed within a detailed cultural setting. An explanatory element is commonly incorporated into the story.

127. Colum, Padraic.
MYTHS OF THE WORLD. 20 engravings by Boriz Artzybasheff. New York, Grosset & Dunlap [1959? c1930] 327 p. (The Universal library, UL–50)   BL310.C55 1959

First published in 1930 under title: *Orpheus: myths of the world.*

Along with the classic myths of the ancient world, this noted poet-storyteller retells the Zuñi myth of the sacred Corn Maidens "who could make grow the plants without which life of flesh cannot flourish." Padraic Colum bases his version of "Paiyatuma and the Maidens of the Corn" on the long, involved account set down by Frank Hamilton Cushing in his "Outlines of Zuñi Creation Myths" (referred to in item 129).

The Kachinas Are Coming *is illustrated with full-color drawings of kachina dolls executed by the author, Gene Meany Hodge. This one, Kwahu (Eagle), embellishes the tale of "Why Kachinas Wear Eagle Feathers." Item 132.*

128. Cushing, Frank H.
 ZUÑI BREADSTUFF. New York, Museum of the American Indian, Heye Foundation, 1920. 673 p. illus., 27 plates (Indian notes and monographs, v. 8) E51.N45, v. 8

Mr. Cushing, who lived with the Zuñi as an adopted member of the tribe from 1879 until 1884, describes in detail the myths, ceremonies, daily customs relating to corn, and Zuñi methods of food production. This material first appeared in a series of articles in the magazine *The Millstone.*

The few tales in this account, told with a satisfying amount of detail and with fully realized plots, reveal the extent to which Zuñi culture is conditioned by the cultivation of maize. In the basic myth relating to the Corn Maidens, these sacred personages are affronted by the flute players and bring suffering upon their people by disappearing. Before they are found, they return in disguised form to leave gifts of food with a faithful old woman and to aid two deserted children. In "The Story of the Young Hunter" Coyote teaches a lazy boy the traditions of his people. The humorous tale of "The Young Men Who Were Fond of Parched Corn and Sweet Gruel, or The Four Awkward

Suitors" is part of the folklore that has grown out of the corn myths
and is told at the winter fireside to amuse the children.

129. Cushing, Frank H., *comp. and tr.*
     ZUÑI FOLK TALES. With a foreword by J. W. Powell and an intro-
     duction by Mary Austin. New York, Knopf, 1931. 474 p. illus.
                                                    E99.Z9C92 1931

These animated Zuñi tales are a delightful source of folklore material.
Eloise Ramsey (item 22) considers this a classic collection "unrivalled
by any later work." Mary Austin, in her appraisal of Mr. Cushing's
literary approach, notes that "all the color and gesture of the time so
delightfully rendered, more than compensate for the occasional lapses
of the translator." While the stories do not conform to the familiar
European folktale pattern, they have drama, humor, and human
interest. The heroes Áhaiyúta and Mátsailéma, twin children of the
Sun-father and the Mother Waters of the World, appear in a few tales.
Mr. Cushing refers the reader to his "Outlines of Zuñi Creation Myths"
in the 13th *Annual Report of the U.S. Bureau of American Ethnology,*
1891/92 (Washington, 1896. U51.U55 13th) p. 321–447, for background on the esoteric tales associated with the Zuñi sacred cosmo-
logical myth.

130. Goodwin, Grenville.
     MYTHS AND TALES OF THE WHITE MOUNTAIN APACHE. New York,
     American Folklore Society, J. J. Augustin, agent, 1939. 223 p.
     (Memoirs of the American Folklore Society, v. 33)
                                                    GR1.A5, v. 33

"A fairly complete collection" of the tales of the White Mountain
Apache of Arizona gathered from native storytellers in the early
1930's. Of particular interest is Mr. Goodwin's discussion of the devices
and techniques used by Indian storytellers. Additional background
information describes the classification of the tales, the literary style,
the function of the tales in Indian society, and important central characters. Included are accounts of the creation, adventures of Coyote
and Big Owl, stories of the "ga·n," who are supernatural beings living
inside mountains and caves, and a group of European tales. Though
this material is not without appeal, it lacks detail in presenting action,
in contrast to the detailed descriptions of various phases of the culture.
The ludicrous situations in the Coyote stories are often cruel and erotic.

131. Harrington, John P., *and* Helen H. Roberts.
     PICURÍS CHILDREN'S STORIES WITH TEXTS AND SONGS. *In* U.S. *Bureau
     of American Ethnology.* Annual report. 43d: 1925/26. Washing-
     ton, 1928. p. 289–447. illus. (incl. music)   E51.U55 43d

Twenty stories gathered in a small mountain village of northeastern New Mexico from a native informant who tells them here just as he heard them from his grandfather and others. Although presented as children's stories, there is nothing to suggest that the tales belong especially to children. In his brief introduction Mr. Harrington notes that the stories were told at the time of the winter solstice and that most of them end with a "good moral teaching or some explanation of nature." Incidents for these short, episodic stories are drawn from the traditional stock—the stolen wife, the deserted children, the successful outcast, and the trickster animal. Tales of ceremonial origins are not included.

This effigy of Tawa (Sun) represents the Sun Father in a story from The Kachinas Are Coming. *Sun Father came to love one of the many Indian maidens upon whom he shone daily. He descended on one of his beams to visit her, took her as his wife, and fathered a son. The maiden, daughter of a village priest, was fearful when the boy was born, so she hid the infant in a nearby valley. He was discovered by a doe and her two fawns and became "The Foster Child of the Deer." This illustration is colored in light blue, yellow, and salmon. Gene Meany Hodge is both author and illustrator. Item 132.*

132. Hodge, Gene M.

THE KACHINAS ARE COMING; PUEBLO INDIAN KACHINA DOLLS WITH RELATED FOLKTALES. Foreword by Frederick W. Hodge. With eighteen color plates of kachina dolls from original drawings by the author. Los Angeles, Steller-Millar, 1936. 129 p.   E99.P9H66

"Works consulted": p. 129.

Fourteen short tales about the sacred kachinas—"lovable and kindly supernaturals which bring rain and other blessings to the people"— are presented in a manner understandable to children. These stories were selected from those originally gathered by Mr. Cushing and other students of Indian folklore. "Notes" to each tale supply additional background information. Mrs. Hodge has illustrated the tales with full-page drawings of the kachina effigies, also referred to as "dolls," which often serve to instruct Indian children in the tribal religion. The stories tell of quarrels among the supernaturals, the trials of a suitor, the fortunes of a deserted child, and the animals' outwitting of the sly Coyote. Many of the tales are characterized by an explanatory element and comment on human nature.

133. Link, Margaret S.

THE POLLEN PATH; A COLLECTION OF NAVAJO MYTHS RETOLD. With a psychological commentary by Joseph L. Henderson. Stanford, Calif., Stanford University Press, 1956. 205 p. illus.   E99.N3L66

Bibliography: p. [203]–205.

A collection of stories for the general reader, taken from the Navaho ritual ceremonies, or chantways—those dramatic rituals centered around a myth known to the medicine man or chanter. Besides her own research, the author has drawn upon original material collected and recorded by Dr. Washington Matthews and others. Through friends, Laura and Sidney Armer, she was introduced to old tribal storytellers. The author states that, for the sake of a clearer outline, she has "remolded" some of the stories. Her treatment of this material is direct and explicit; sometimes she eliminates details and incidents from a long repetitive series of episodes and summarizes others. Important are the stories of heroes who journey to the world of the gods, pass tests or overcome obstacles, and return to their people with valuable knowledge. The appearance of the Coyote stories here is explained in the preface as being connected to the religious rites in the "evil or 'not-good' aspect of these chantways." Included are many of the familiar trickster adventures of Coyote. Useful descriptive and explanatory material on the Navaho chantways, their pantheon of gods, songs, and sandpainting is contained in the appendix. Dr. Henderson's essay is offered as a psychological interpretation of mythology.

134. Lloyd, John W.

AW-AW-TAM INDIAN NIGHTS; BEING THE MYTHS AND LEGENDS OF
THE PIMAS OF ARIZONA. As received by J. William Lloyd from
Comalk-Hawk-Kih (Thin Buckskin) thru the interpretation of
Edward H. Wood. Westfield, N.J., The Lloyd Group [c1911]
241 p. port.   E99.P6L7

Mr. Lloyd lived with the Pima Indians for two months in the summer
of 1903 in order to record these stories as they were dictated by a
trained tribal historian, whose nephew then translated them into
English. A section of explanatory notes and additional background
information follows each tale.

135. Matthews, Washington.

NAVAHO LEGENDS. With introduction, notes, illustrations, texts,
interlinear translations, and melodies. Boston, Published for the
American Folklore Society, by Houghton, Mifflin, 1897. 299 p.
illus. (incl. col. plates), double map. (Memoirs of the American
Folklore Society, v. 5)   GR1.A5, v. 5

"Bibliographic notes. By Frederick Webb Hodge": p. [276]–278.

The "Navaho Origin Legend" and two rite-myths, collected and translated by Washington Matthews, are presented with introductory background information. The translation of the tales, which were narrated
by medicine men "in fluent Navaho" and are "of such literary perfec-
tion as to hold the hearer's attention," retains the spirit of the originals,
but not the exact words. The "Navaho Origin Legend" is arranged
in four distinct parts: 1. "The Story of the Emergence," 2. "Early
Events in the Fifth World," 3. "The War Gods," and 4. "Growth of
the Navaho Nation." Mr. Matthews considers the rite-myths, "Natī'-
nesthani" and "The Great Shell of Kīntyél," to be "among the most
interesting and ingenious that have been collected among the Nava-
hoes"—the moral of the latter being that the poor and humble must
not be despised. The compiler adds a note to the literary borrower:

He begs that the latter will not garble or distort what is here written,—that he
will not put alien thoughts into the minds of these pagan heroes; that he will not
arm them with the weapons nor clothe them in the habiliments of an alien race;
that he will not make them act incongruous parts.

136. Opler, Morris E.

MYTHS AND TALES OF THE CHIRICAHUA APACHE INDIANS. With an
appendix of ·Apache and Navaho comparative references by
David French. [New York, American Folklore Society] 1942.
114 p. (Memoirs of the American Folklore Society, v. 37, 1942)
                                                              GR1.A5, v. 37

Bibliography: p. 112–114.

Material gathered during three anthropological field trips to the Mescalero Reservation in New Mexico in the years 1931–35. Footnotes contain background information for the tales and summaries of variants not given in full. The motif index prepared by Mr. French brings together references to show the distribution among the various Apache tribes and the Navaho of the myths and tales found in this collection. Of the Chiricahua Apache folklore Mr. Opler states, "We are dealing here with a living literature, dramatic and satisfying to its audience, capable of modification and growth in response to changing conditions." This is evident in the number of elements derived from European folklore and in the Coyote episodes that satirize the Indian's relationship with the white man.

137. ———.
    MYTHS AND TALES OF THE JICARILLA APACHE INDIANS. New York, American Folklore Society, G. E. Stechert, agents, 1938. 406 p. (Memoirs of the American Folklore Society, v. 31)
                                              GR1.A5, v. 31

So rich is Jicarilla Apache mythology, says the compiler, that the material presented here, as recorded between the spring of 1934 and the spring of 1935, offers only a "representative picture." The editor briefly describes the type of material not included and then discusses the tales and their educative role as an accurate guide to behavior, beliefs, and ceremonies. Despite the weight of cultural details and realistic descriptions of everyday occurrences, these tales have a lively freshness of expression—as in the reaction of the Indians who see the sun for the first time in "The People Who Went to the North":

    The first time they peeped over the rim and saw the sun they were afraid. They said, "That is a monster with a big eye."

138. Parsons, Elsie (Clews), *ed.*
    TEWA TALES. New York, American Folklore Society, G. E. Stechert, agents, 1926. 304 p. (Memoirs of the American Folklore Society, v. 19)
                                      GR1.A5, v. 19

"List of references": p. [303]–304.

Folktales from the Tewa Indians of New Mexico and Arizona. Dr. Parsons discusses outside influences on Pueblo folklore and the "acculturated tale." She notes that the "Pueblo novelistic type of tale, distinctive in Indian folklore, has certainly been influenced by, it may have developed from, the Hispanic or European type of 'fairy tale.' " The majority of stories in this collection tells of the deceived or deserted youth, or of the rejected suitor who overcomes supernatural powers with the aid of friendly animals and magical devices. Olivella Flower boy, the corn girls, Spider old woman, and Coyote old man frequently appear as the central tale personages in this authentic source of potentially good storytelling material.

139. Russell, Frank.
THE PIMA INDIANS. *In* U.S. *Bureau of American Ethnology.* Annual report. 26th: 1904/05. Washington, 1908. p. 3–389. illus.
E51.U55 26th

A full account of the ethnology of the Pima tribe on the Gila River Reservation in southern Arizona, based on material gathered in the early 1900's. Following a brief description of the traditions relating to tribal lore are a long version of the Pima creation myth and a group of "Nursery Tales"—humorous episodes in which Coyote is outwitted by other animals. The creation myth depicts the accomplishments of Earth Doctor, Elder Brother, Coyote, and South Doctor in making the world and its people, and their struggles with cannibal monsters. The account of Väntre, the gambler transformed into an eagle, and many other incidents related here are found in editions for children.

140. White, Leslie A.
THE ACOMA INDIANS. *In* U.S. *Bureau of American Ethnology.* Annual report. 47th; 1929/30. Washington, 1932. p. 17–192. illus.
E51.U55 47th
GN2.U5 47th
Bibliography: p. 191–192.

The 17 tales printed in this report, a few of them recorded in broken English and told in a contemporary narrative style, reveal the teller's imaginative gift. Dr. White's description of the Acoma pantheon is a good source of authentic background material. Included are some of the stories retold in *The Dancing Horses of Acoma* (item 145).

Children's Editions

141. Cuadra Downing, Orlando, *ed.*
THE ADVENTURES OF DON COYOTE; AMERICAN INDIAN FOLK TALES. New York, Exposition Press [1955] 100 p.   E98.F6C87

The stories in this collection first appeared in *Pueblo Indian Folk-*

Earth Magician, dissatisfied with the world he has created, pulls the bowl of the sky down upon the earth. From "Why the World Is the Way It Is" in Indian Tales of the Desert People, *compiled by William D. Hayes and illustrated with his line drawings. Item 143.*

Stories, by Charles Lummis (item 147), *The Seven Cities of Cibola,* by Aileen Nusbaum (item 148), and *Navajo Winter Nights; Folk Tales and Myths of the Navajo People,* by Dorothy Hogner (item 144). Reprinted with only minor changes and without illustrations, the tales form a serviceable compilation for the storyteller.

142. De Huff, Elizabeth W.
    TAYTAY'S TALES. Illustrations by Fred Kabotie and Otis Polelonema. New York, Harcourt, Brace [c1922] 213 p.   E98.F6D3

The compiler gathered from Indian men and children 46 authentic Pueblo folktales that are usually told to the children by the Indian Taytay, or grandfather. In her preface Mrs. De Huff adds a note to explain, from the Indian's point of view, the element of cruelty that

"Who are you and where do you come from?" asked the Black Monster. Nils Hogner's illustration for the tale of "The Great Flood" from Navajo Winter Nights, *written by Dorothy Childs Hogner. Item 144.*

appears in the tales. In the preparation of this collection, advice and criticism from Mary Austin are acknowledged. The pueblo from which each story was secured is identified after the title. Explanatory notes, in a final section, cover such topics as "Time of Tale-Telling," "Songs," and "Ceremonies, Commonly Known as Indian Dances." Mr. Fox appears as the most prominent character; others are Coyote, Grandmother Spider, and Man-Eater. Most are animal trickster tales, but a few are about witchcraft and monstrous beings. Straightforward retellings in short sentences are enlivened by dialogue and the music and words of animals' songs. The small ink drawings and watercolors are by two Hopi Indian boys.

This collection was followed by a second, *Taytay's Memories,* by Elizabeth W. De Huff (New York, Harcourt, Brace [c1924] 255 p. illus. E98.F6D28).

143. Hayes, William D.
      INDIAN TALES OF THE DESERT PEOPLE. New York, McKay [c1957]
      110 p.   E98.F6H54

Twelve tales based on ancestral lore of the Pima and Papago Indians of the Gila River and the Salt River valleys in the desert country that is now south central Arizona. The compiler cites as sources collections made by Frank Russell (item 139) and John Lloyd (item 134). Mr. Hayes states that in order to make these tales appealing to young readers he elaborated incidents, provided logical motives, and supplied descriptions of the desert and mountains. He limited his selection to those stories that relate to the creation and explain how things came to be as they are now. The account of "Man-Eagle" ends with the modern explanation recorded by Mr. Russell. The book is illustrated with lively line drawings.

144. Hogner, Dorothy C.
      NAVAJO WINTER NIGHTS; FOLK TALES AND MYTHS OF THE NAVAJO
      PEOPLE. Pictures by Nils Hogner. New York, Nelson, 1935. 180 p.
                                                         E99.N3H65

A Navaho medicine man and interpreter related many of these tales to the Hogners. In the preface Mrs. Hogner explains that she has added descriptions of the Navaho and their country to this "authentic" material to make it more attractive to young readers. She has arranged the tales in four groups: "Tales of Very, Very, Very, Long Ago," "Big Long Man's Stories," "How Stories," and "Tales of Coyote, the Schemer." The narratives in the first group are based on the Navaho's sacred origin myth. A summary of the Navaho's concept of the emergence adds understanding and enjoyment to the adventures of the two War Gods who battle monsters and giants and bring the

One of the Tewa Firelight
Tales, by Ahlee James,
describes a four-day visit made
to White Flower Town by the
god Montezuma, called
Pasayawoo by more northern
Tewa Indians. He showed
the villagers how to hunt
big game and he taught them
the Buffalo Dance. Among
the dancers, drawn by
Awa Tsireh, is one repre-
senting the hunters. Next are
two "dancers dressed as deer
with antlers, that stalk
forward on four legs, the front
legs being supplied by rods
held in the hands of the men
who represent those animals."
At the far right is one of
the little boy antelopes who
"also trip in with . . . little
forefeet, managed as the deer
manage theirs." Item 146.

horse as a gift to their people. The tales of Big Long Man follow a
more familiar European folktale pattern. The last two groups include
the "how and why" stories and the trickster tales of Coyote, Deer,
Badger, Porcupine, and others. A well-selected choice of incidents
from the stories have been illustrated in simple black-and-white, full-
page, line drawings.

145. Hunt, Wolf R.
THE DANCING HORSES OF ACOMA, AND OTHER ACOMA INDIAN
STORIES. Cleveland, World Pub. Co. [1963] 163 p.   E99.A16H8

In a concluding "Note About the Acoma" Helen Rushmore says that
these tales, recorded by Mr. Hunt, an Acoma chief, are some that
delighted him as a child. They have been retold in a familiar fairytale
style but are closely identified with their desert environment and the
Acoma's concern for rain. The predominance of human heroes aided
by supernatural powers and friendly animals, and the number of
stories about giants enhance the appeal of this folklore for children.
The full-page watercolor illustrations are done in an "authentic Indian
flat style."

146. James, Ahlee.
TEWA FIRELIGHT TALES. With illustrations by Awa Tsireh and others. New York, Longmans, Green, 1927. 248 p.   E99.T35J28

Tewa myths, traditionally told on winter evenings, were gathered by the author during a 3-year residence in the village of San Ildefonso, New Mexico. The Indian storyteller or Indian translator is identified. Primarily hero stories, these retellings have a familiar fairytale quality, though in broad outline they follow versions in Dr. Parsons' collection (item 138) and incorporate typical Indian characters and magical devices. The emergence myth and ceremonial tales are not represented, and the small selection of animal tales includes some of European origin. The full-page color illustrations of masked dancers and incidents from the stories were drawn by Indian artists.

147. Lummis, Charles F.
PUEBLO INDIAN FOLK-STORIES. New York, Century, 1910. 257 p. illus.   E99.P9L96

Published in 1894 under title: *The Man Who Married the Moon*.

To the music of flutes sighing like the wind, masked Páiyatuma—the God of Dew—and Maidens of the House of the Stars dance in the Cave of the Rain-

bow. From "The Gift of the Flutes" in The Seven Cities of Cibola *by Aileen Nusbaum; illustrated by Margaret Finnan. Item 148.*

Thirty-three stories from the Tewa pueblo of Isleta, New Mexico, where the compiler lived for five years. They are written simply and presented as if told around an Indian campfire, with background information preceding each tale and in footnotes. The narrative style is smooth except when interrupted by the use of both the Indian and English forms of a word. The stories tell of Coyote, often the victim of his own jokes, and of false friends, rejected suitors, the Yellow-Corn-Maidens, who use the magic hoop to snare their victims in order to transform them, and other witches. Also included are true adventures into which a supernatural element is introduced and modern tales of Spanish origin. This collection, unattractive in format, is still a useful source of storytelling material.

148. Nusbaum, Aileen.
   THE SEVEN CITIES OF CIBOLA. With pictures by Margaret Finnan. New York, Putnam, 1926. 167 p.   PZ8.1.N80Se

Also published with title: *Zuñi Indian Tales*.

The author, whose husband was a field assistant during the excavation of Háwikuh, one of the seven cities of Cibola, heard these stories being related to her young son by the old men of the tribe. As her main sources of information she cites Mr. Cushing's "Outlines of Zuñi Creation Myths" (item 129), *Zuñi Folk Tales* (item 129), and *Zuñi Breadstuff* (item 128). This varied, well-chosen group of tales introduces such important tale personages as the War-Gods, the dreadful cannibal demons, Kolowissi (Serpent of the Sea), and the Maidens of

Corn. Also here are some of the most appealing of the animal tales.
Stories have been shortened, detailed descriptions of the culture have
been omitted, and some explanations more satisfactory to a child have
been supplied. The full-page color illustrations and border decorations
are based on authentic Zuñi designs, costumes, and customs. Eloise
Ramsey says of this collection, "The book may be counted among the
few collections of Indian tales intended for boys and girls which was
made in the right way" (item 22).

149. Peck, Leigh.
    DON COYOTE. Illustrated by Virginia L. Burton. Boston, Hough-
    ton Mifflin, 1942. 78 p.   PZ8.1.P335Do

Stories about Coyote, "this wisest of animals," told by Indians and
Mexicans. These modern versions are introduced by a description of
the true coyote, which explains why it is such a popular figure in the
folklore of the Southwest. Although most of the stories have a Mexican
flavor, "Coyote Changes His Coat," "Coyote Is Tricked at Last," and
"How Coyote Flew with the Blackbirds" are more representative of
the North American Indian. This collection stands as a good example
of living folklore presented in a very attractive manner with colorful,
lively drawings. No sources are given, but these most popular of all

*"Often the den was several rooms, one for the father, one for the mother, and
one or more nurseries for the pups." Illustration by Virginia Lee Burton from
Don Coyote by Leigh Peck. Item 149.*

Choo-Kutt the Owl and Haw-aw-Aux, a wicked giantess, characters in the legend "Little-White-Feather," as depicted by Katherine F. Kitt. From Long Ago Told Legends of the Papago Indians, *collected by the artist and arranged by Harold Bell Wright. Item 151.*

Facing page, a halftitle from Navaho Tales *by William Whitman 3rd features Spider Woman. Illustrator, John P. Heins. Item 150.*

tales are readily found in the collections described for this culture area.
  "Coyote Is Tricked at Last" opens:

One bright, sunny day Coyote went hunting. The warmth of the sun had brought an old Locust out, too, from his hiding place in the earth. Locust crawled up on one of the branches of an old mountain pine, and hooked his feet into the bark. Then he began to play his fiddle and to sing:

> "Locust, locust, fiddling a tune!
> Locust, locust singing a tune!
> High up on the pine tree bough,
> Tightly clinging,
> Fiddling a tune!
> Singing a tune!"

"Delight of my ears," cried Coyote, "how beautiful your song is!"

150. Whitman, William.

NAVAHO TALES, retold by William Whitman 3rd. With illustrations by John P. Heins. Boston, Houghton Mifflin, 1925. 217 p.

E99.N3W6

Faithful versions of stories originally translated by Dr. Washington Matthews (item 135). The story of the emergence contains much that is mysterious, and the telling is very moving. There is poetic beauty in the long narrative of the War Gods' battles to rid the world of monsters, aided variously by friendly animals, forces of nature, and wisdom. In the War Gods' final quest against Old Age, Cold Woman, Poverty, and Hunger, Spider Woman gives them a magic formula:

"Put down your feet with pollen. Put down your hands with pollen. Put down your head with pollen. Then your feet are at peace; your hands are at peace; your body is at peace; your mind is at peace; your voice is at peace. The trail is one of beauty. Be still."

The three remaining tales are of heroes who acquire valuable knowledge that they bring back to their people. Striking black-and-white silhouette drawings illustrate the tales.

151. Wright, Harold B.

LONG AGO TOLD (HUH-KEW AH-KAH) LEGENDS OF THE PAPAGO INDIANS. Illustrated by Katherine F. Kitt. London, New York, D. Appleton, 1929. 289 p. E99.P25W94

Quiet retellings of the tales of the Papago, an agricultural tribe of the desert. They are presented in a coherent, simple, storytelling prose from fragments that a number of native storytellers related to the book's illustrator, a friend of the Papago. The tales are closely identified with the tribe's desert environment and reflect constant concern for crops, a need for rain, and for vigilance against unfriendly animals. Instructing, rewarding, and punishing his people, the Great Spirit (Eé-e-toy) appears in many forms. Such popular themes as the theft of fire and the rejected suitor are woven into the myths.

THE QUEST OF THE WAR GODS

Po-o-canu's illustration for "The Witch Wife," from Tewa Firelight Tales *by Ahlee James. Item 146.*

152. Zitkala-Sa.
OLD INDIAN LEGENDS. With illustrations by Angel de Cora (Hinook-Mahiwi-Kilinaka) Boston, Ginn, 1901. 165 p. plates.
PZ8.1.Z69O

American name: Gertrude Bonnin.

Retellings of the adventures of Iktomi the snare weaver and Iya the eater, which the author heard from old Dakota storytellers. These 14 tales convey the charm of Indian folklore, though they are not presented in an Indian narrative style. The terms "fairy" and "imp" are used to describe the wily spider who appears in the guise of a Dakota brave, outwits the ducks by leading them in a "merry dance-song," and is punished for his selfishness by the great stone god Inyan.

Numbers refer to entries, not pages.

Abnaki, 112
Achomawi, 78
Acoma, 140, 145
The Acoma Indians, 140
The Adventures of Don Coyote,
   141
Alabama, 123
The Alaskan Eskimos, 36
Alaskan Igloo Tales, 40
Alexander, Hartley B., 1
Algic Researches, 101
Algonkin, 103–104, 109, 113
*The Algonquin Legends of
   New England,* 109, 114
The American Indian, 10
*An Analysis of Coeur d'Alene
   Indian Myths,* 49
Apache, 130, 136–137
Assiniboin, 98
Aw-au-tam Indian Nights, 134
Ayre, Robert, 3a, 63

Badger, the Mischief Maker, 112
Bailey, Carolyn S., 124
Barbeau, Charles M., 63, 96, 107
Barrett, Samuel A., 69
Bayliss, Clara (Kern), 37
Beck, Horace P., 108
Bell, Corydon, 125
Bellabella, 54, 56, 67
Bella Bella Tales, 54, 67
Benedict, Ruth F., 126
Beyond the Clapping Mountains,
   38
Beyond the High Hills, 30

*A Bibliography of North Ameri-
   can Folklore and Folksong,* 20
Birket-Smith, Kaj, 31, 42
Blackfeet, 44, 64, 86, 89–90, 105,
   113
Blackfeet Indian Stories, 89
Blackfoot Lodge Tales, 81, 89
Block, Gwendoline H., 71
Boas, Franz, 2, 24–26, 37, 40a,
   45–46, 50, 52, 54–56, 63,
   66–67
The Box of Daylight, 66
Burlin, Natalie (Curtis), 11
By Cheyenne Campfires, 82

Calapooya. *See* Kalapuya
California Indian Folklore, 74
*California Indian Nights Enter-
   tainments,* 71
Canadian Fairy Tales, 113
Canadian Wonder Tales, 113
The Caribou Eskimos, 31
Caswell, Helen R., 37a
The Central Eskimo, 24, 37
Chamberlain, Alexander, 46
Chapman, John W., 43
Cherokee, 119–122, 124–125a
Cherokee Animal Tales, 125a
The Cheyenne, 79
Cheyenne, 79, 82, 95
Chinook, 57
Chipewyan, 42, 44
Chippewa (Ojibwa), 90, 97,
   104–106
Choate, Florence, 101

122

Clackamas, 57
Clark, Ella E., 12, 47
Clay, Charles, 87
Coeur d'Alene, 45, 49
Coffin, Tristram P., 13
Colum, Padraic, 127
Connelley, William E., 96
*Contemporary Problems of
   Folklore Collecting,* 4
*The Content and Style of an Oral
   Literature,* 57
*Contributions to Chipewyan
   Ethnology,* 42
Converse, Harriet (Maxwell), 115
Coos, 58
Coos Myth Texts, 58
Cowlitz, 61
Coyote Stories, 53
Cree, 44, 87, 90, 105
Creeks, 123
Cris. *See* Cree
Crow, 84, 91
Cuadra Downing, Orlando, 141
The Culture of the Winnebago,
   100
Curry, Jane L., 77
Curtin, Jeremiah, 70, 116–117
Curtis, Edward S., 14
Curtis, Elizabeth, 101
Cushing, Frank H., 127–129,
   132, 148

Dakota, 152
The Dancing Horses of Acoma,
   140, 145
Davis, John B., 119
Davis, Susan B., 104
The Dawn of the World, 75
The Day Tuk Became a Hunter,
   40a
De Huff, Elizabeth W., 142
Dog-Ribs, 44
Don Coyote, 149
Dorsey, George A., 79, 80

*Down From the Lonely Moun-
   tain,* 77
Dundes, Alan, 3
Duvall, D. C., 86

The Eagle's Gift, 41
Eastman, Charles A., 88
Egoff, Sheila A., 3a
The Eskimo About Bering Strait,
   27, 37
Eskimo Folk-Tales, 28
*The Eskimo of Baffin Land
   and Hudson Bay,* 26
*European Tales Among the
   North American Indians,* 8

Farrand, Livingston, 45
Feldmann, Susan, 15
Fisher, Anne (Benson), 78
Flancs-de-chien. *See* Dog-Ribs
*Folklore for Children and Young
   People,* 22
*Folklore of the Menomini
   Indians,* 103
The Folktale, 9
Folk-Tales of Salishan and
   Sahaptin Tribes, 45, 49, 52
Frachtenberg, Leo J., 59
Friends of Thunder, 121

Gabrielino, 78
Garfield, Viola E., 4
Gatschet, Albert S., 59
Gifford, Edward W., 71
Gillham, Charles E., 38–39
Glooscap and His Magic, 3a, 112
Glooscap the Great Chief, 114
Glooskap's Country, 113
Gluskap the Liar, 108
Goodwin, Grenville, 130
Gould, Marian K., 45
Grinnell, George B., 64, 81–83, 89

Haida, 65
*Handbook of American Indians
   North of Mexico,* 5

Handbook of the Indians of
  California, 72
Hare, 44
Harrington, John P., 131
Harris, Christie, 3a, 65
Hayes, William D., 143
Haywood, Charles, 20
Hewitt, John N. B., 116
Hill, Kay, 3a, 112
Hillyer, William H., 66
Hitchiti, 123
Hodge, Frederick W., 5
Hodge, Gene M., 132
Hogner, Dorothy C., 141, 144
Hooke, Hilda M., 17
Hopi, 142
Hunt, Wolf R., 145
Huron, 96
Huron and Wyandot Mythology,
  96, 107

Igloo Tales, 40
The Indian Fairy Book, 101
Indian Legends From Algic
  Researches, 101
Indian Legends From the
  Northern Rockies, 47
Indian Legends of Canada, 12
Indian Lodge-Fire Stories, 90
Indian Myths, 96
Indian Old-Man Stories, 90
Indian Tales of North America,
  13
Indian Tales of the Desert People,
  143
Indian Why Stories, 90
The Indians' Book, 11
The Indians of Canada, 6
Indians on Horseback, 92
Ingalik. See Ten'a
The Inland Whale, 73
Intellectual Culture of the Copper
  Eskimos, 34
Intellectual Culture of the
  Hudson Bay Eskimos, 32

Iroquois, 115–116, 118

Jacobs, Melville, 57–61, 68
James, Ahlee, 146
Jarrett, Robert F., 120
Jenness, Diamond, 6, 63
John Rattling-Gourd of Big Cove,
  125
Journal of American Folklore,
  13, 21

The Kachinas Are Coming, 132
Kalapuya, 59
Kalapuya Texts, 59
Karok, 76, 78
Kawchottine. See Hare
Keithahn, Edward L., 40
Kilpatrick, Anna G., 121
Kilpatrick, Jack F., 121
Kiowa, 85, 92–93
Kiowa Tales, 85
Kittitas, 61
Klickitat, 61
Koasati, 123
Kootenai Why Stories, 51
Kroeber, Alfred L., 72
Kroeber, Theodora, 73
Kulóskap the Master, 109, 114
Kutenai, 46, 51
Kutenai Tales, 46
Kwakiutl, 55, 65, 67
Kwakiutl Tales, 55, 67

Latta, Frank F., 74
Leach, Maria, 18
Leekley, Thomas B., 105
Legends of the Micmacs, 110, 114
Leland, Charles G., 109, 112, 114
Linderman, Frank B., 46, 51,
  90–91
Link, Margaret S., 133
Literary Aspects of North
  American Mythology, 7
Lloyd, John W., 134, 143

124   Long Ago Told, 151
Longfellow, Henry Wadsworth,
    101
Loucheux, 44
Lowie, Robert H., 84
Lummis, Charles F., 141, 147

The Mackenzie Eskimos, 35
Macmillan, Cyrus, 113
The Man Who Married the
    Moon, 147
Marriott, Alice L., 92–93
Martin, Frances G., 48, 52, 67
Mathews, Cornelius, 101
Matthews, Washington, 133, 135,
    150
Medicine Men of Hooper Bay, 39
Melzack, Ronald, 40a
Menominee, 103
Merriam, Clinton H., 75, 78
Micmac, 109–110, 114
The Millstone, 128
Miwok, 74–75, 78
Modoc, 70
Mono, 78
Mooney, James, 119–122, 125a
The Morphology of North Ameri-
    can Indian Folktales, 3
Motif-Index of Folk-Literature, 23
Mourning Dove, 53
The Myth of Hiawatha, 101–102
Mythology of the Blackfoot, 86
Myths and Legends of the
    New York Iroquois, 115
Myths and Tales of the Chiri-
    cahua Apache Indians, 136
Myths and Tales of the Jicarilla
    Apache Indians, 137
Myths and Tales of the South-
    eastern Indians, 123
Myths and Tales of the White
    Mountain Apache, 130
Myths and Traditions of the
    Crow Indians, 84
Myths of the Cherokee, 122

Myths of the Modocs, 70
Myths of the World, 127

Nakotcho-kutchin. See Loucheux
Natchez, 123
Navaho, 133, 135–136, 141, 144,
    150
Navaho Legends, 135
Navaho Tales, 150
Navajo Winter Nights, 141, 144
Nelson, Edward W., 27, 37
The Netsilik Eskimos, 33
Nez Percé, 45, 48, 52
Nez Percé Texts, 48, 52
Nine Tales of Coyote, 48, 52
Nine Tales of Raven, 67
Nootka, 56
The North American Indian, 14
North American [Mythology], 1
Northwest Sahaptin Texts, 60–61
Ntlakyapamuk. See Thompson
    River Indians
Nusbaum, Aileen, 141, 148

Occoneechee, 120
Ojibwa. See Chippewa
Okanagon, 45, 53
Olcott, Frances J., 19
Old Indian Legends, 152
Old Man Coyote (Crow), 91
Once Upon a Totem, 3a, 65
Oneóta, 101
Opler, Morris E., 136–137
Orpheus: Myths of the World,
    127
Ottawa, 105
"Outlines of Zuñi Creation
    Myths," 127, 129, 148

Pahute Indian Legends, 94
Paiute, 94
Palmer, William R., 94
Papago, 143, 151
Parker, Arthur C., 115, 118

Parsons, Elsie (Clews), 85, 138, 146
Partridge, Emelyn N., 114
Passamaquoddy, 109
Pawnee, 64, 80, 83
Pawnee Hero Stories and Folk-Tales, 83
Peaux-de-Lièvre. *See* Hare
Peck, Leigh, 149
Pend d'Oreille, 45
Penney, Grace J., 95
Penobscot, 108–109, 111
Penobscot Transformer Tales, 111
Petitot, Émile F., 44
Phinney, Archie, 48, 52
Picurís Children's Stories With Texts and Songs, 131
Pieds-Noirs. *See* Blackfeet
Pima, 134, 139, 143
The Pima Indians, 139
The Pollen Path, 133
Pomo, 69, 78
Pomo Myths, 69
Powers, Stephen, 76
Prince, John D., 109, 114
Pueblo, 126, 132, 138, 141–142
Pueblo Indian Folk-Stories, 141, 147
The Punishment of the Stingy, 64

Race, Language and Culture, 2
Radin, Paul, 7, 97–100
The Rainbow Book of American Folk Tales and Legends, 18
Ramsey, Eloise, 22
Rand, Silas T., 109–110, 112, 114
Rasmussen, Knud J. V., 28, 30, 32–36, 40a–41
The Red Indian Fairy Book, 19
Reichard, Gladys A., 49
Reid, Dorothy M., 3a, 106
The Republic of Childhood, 3a
Rink, Hinrich J., 29
Roberts, Helen H., 131
Rumbling Wings, 118

Running, Corinne, 68
Russell, Frank, 139, 143

Sanpoil, 45
Santiam, 59
Satterlee, John V., 103
Saynday's People, 92
Scheer, George F., 125a
Schoolcraft, Henry R., 101–102, 104
Seneca, 116–118
Seneca Fiction, Legends, and Myths, 116
Seneca Indian Myths, 117
Seneca Myths and Folk Tales, 118
The Seven Cities of Cibola, 141, 148
Shadows from the Singing House, 37a
Sioux, 88
Sketco, the Raven, 3a, 63
Skinner, Alanson B., 103
Skunny Wundy, 118
Smoky Day's Wigwam Evenings, 88
Some Cherokee Stories, 119
Some Myths and Tales of the Ojibwa of Southeastern Ontario, 97
Song of Hiawatha, 101
Speck, Frank G., 111
Spinden, Herbert J., 45
Stories California Indians Told, 78
Stories From an Indian Cave, 124
The Storytelling Stone, 15
Swampy Cree Legends, 87
Swanton, John R., 62, 67, 121, 123

Tales and Traditions of the Eskimo, 29
Tales of Nanabozho, 3a, 106
Tales of the Bark Lodges, 107
Tales of the Cheyennes, 95

126   *Tales of the North American Indians*, 16

Taytay's Tales, 142

Tchiglit. *See* Tlingit

Tchippewyan. *See* Chipewyan

Teit, James A., 45, 50, 63

Ten'a, 43

Ten'a Texts and Tales From Anvik, Alaska, 43

Tewa, 138, 146–147

Tewa Firelight Tales, 146

Tewa Tales, 138

Thlingchadinne. *See* Dog-Ribs

Thompson River Indians, 45, 50

Thompson, Stith, 8–9, 16, 23

Thule Expedition, 30, 41

Thunder in the Mountains, 17

Tlingit, 44, 50, 65, 67, 98

Tlingit Myths and Texts, 62, 67

Traditions Indiennes du Canada Nord-Ouest, 44

Traditions of the Skidi Pawnee, 80

Traditions of the Thompson River Indians of British Columbia, 50

A Treasury of Eskimo Tales, 37

Tribes of California, 76

The Trickster, 98

Tsimishian, 50, 55–56, 65, 67

Tsimshian Mythology, 56, 67

Walker, Bertrand N. O., 107

Webster, Helen L., 110

When Coyote Walked the Earth, 68

White, Leslie A., 140

Whitman, William, 150

Why the North Star Stands Still, 94

Williams, Mentor L., 101

Winnebago, 98–100

Winnebago Hero Cycles, 99

Winter-Telling Stories, 85, 92–93

Wisconsin Lore for Boys and Girls, 104

Wissler, Clark, 10, 86

The World of Manabozho, 105

Wright, Harold B., 151

Wyandot, 96, 107

Yokuts, 74, 78

Zitkala-Sa, 152

Zuñi, 126–129, 148

Zuñi Breadstuff, 128, 148

Zuñi Folk Tales, 129, 148

Zuñi Indian Tales, 148

Zuni Mythology, 126

☆ U.S. GOVERNMENT PRINTING OFFICE: 1969 O — 312-3111